A Basic Cours

in

Manual

Communication

published by the

Communicative Skills Program

Terrence J. O'Rourke, Director

Illustrated by:
Donald W. Lacock, Manager
Educational Development
Audio Visual Center
University of Iowa
Iowa City, Iowa

Consultants:
Harold J. Domich, Associate Professor
Rex P. Lowman, Associate Professor
Gallaudet College
Washington, D.C.
Shirley H. Glassman, Sign Language Instructor
Philadelphia High Schools, Extension Program
and
Philadelphia Hearing Society

Revision art by:
Shirley A. Hoemann
Bowling Green, Ohio

This publication was supported, in part, by Grant RSA 44-P-81003/3-01 from the Department of Health, Education, and Welfare, Social and Rehabilitation Service, Rehabilitation Services Administration.

First Edition Oct. 1970
2nd printing May 1972
3rd printing Nov. 1972
4th printing Jan. 1973

Second Edition Sept. 1973
2nd printing Nov. 1974
3rd printing June 1975
5th printing Oct. 1976
6th printing March 1977
7th printing November 1977
8th printing June 1978
9th printing September 1978
10th printing February 1979
11th printing March 1979
12th printing July 1979
13th printing February 1980
14th printing December 1980
15th printing June 1981
16th printing January 1982
17th printing March 1983
18th printing November 1983
19th printing April 1984
20th printing August 1985
21st printing October1986
22nd printing October 1987
23rd printing June 1989
24th printing February 1990
25th printing July 1990
26th printing July 1991
27th printing 1992
28th printing 1993
29th printing 1994
30th printing 1995
31st printing 1997

DEDICATION

To all the O'Rourkes:

> Rose McEvoy
> Wilfred Hugh Sr.
> John Francis
> Wilfred Hugh Jr.
> Bernard Vincent
> Dennis Eugene
> Betty Holtzclaw
> Kathleen Sue
> Michael Kevin
> Terrence Patrick

FOREWORD

Three years ago, I wrote the foreword for the first edition of "A Basic Course in Manual Communication," expecting that to last for a long, long time. But the language of signs, like any other language, is a living thing, subject to change, improvement and growth. This is perhaps more true of the language of signs than for other languages due to its suppression throughout the past 100 years.

In the first edition, we noted the contributions of the District of Columbia Association of the Deaf and the input from its teachers, and the teachers on the staff of the Communicative Skills Program that made the book possible.

We also noted that through the years there had been a "constant revision and refinement of teaching techniques and materials, all of which is reflected here." This holds true and is the reason for this first revision of a text that is but three years old. Included are certain elements that have come into wide use in recent years. The NAD does not necessarily endorse these elements but does acknowledge its responsibility to provide the student with the most modern and comprehensive textbook it can.

Frederick C. Schreiber
Executive Secretary
National Association of the Deaf

September 1973
814 Thayer Avenue
Silver Spring, Maryland 20910

INTRODUCTION

The revised edition of *A Basic Course in Manual Communication* follows essentially the same format as the original text. However, close to 200 new illustrations have been added to the revised edition, all bibliographies have been updated, and practice exercises have also been changed. Thus, the revised edition constitutes a new text, in keeping with the Communicative Skills Program philosophy of providing the most current material available on manual communication that is beyond the realm of experimentation.

Two new features are included within this volume: 1.) an appendix that provides some of the newer signs for pronouns, affixes, articles, etc. where previously no signs were recognized. While the NAD does not endorse these signs for general usage, they are receiving fairly wide-spread acceptance within many school programs and are provided here as a convenience to the student; 2.) a bibliography of books related to deafness that would be of interest to any serious student of manual communication.

Transparency masters corresponding to the 737 illustrations in the revised edition are *not* available because of the new numbers assigned to illustrations in the text and the large number of new drawings. Those seeking reinforcement for classroom instruction are advised to avail themselves of the flash card packs developed by Harry Hoemann of Bowling Green State University and available for $10.95 per pack from the NAD. The pack contains 500 drawings and verbal descriptions of over 1300 signs. They have been developed as an excellent supplement to the revised text in co-operation with the author.

As in the original text, all illustrations are in one section of the text and practice exercises in another. The practice exercises are designed to allow for progressive reinforcement of acquired vocabulary. Those words set in italics are a part of the vocabulary that has previously been taught and the student should be able to give the sign for the italicized words. Words set in Roman type may be fingerspelled. Students should, however, be encouraged to use all the signs that they know.

The "DM" notation in parenthesis on a number of illustrations represents "double movement". In many instances the repetition of a sign changes the meaning. For example, the sign representing "clean", as in "He put on a *clean* shirt", is made by a single outward movement of the right palm over the left. When this movement is repeated, however, it becomes "cleaning" as in "She is *cleaning* the house". Some signs, such as "look for" require a double movement in making the basic sign.

As an aid to instructors, additional words have been added and indexed for various concept-related signs. It would be impossible, however, to list all those English words that can be used to translate a sign. It remains for the teacher to show the student how to select signs according to meaning when interpreting. To aid somewhat in this area the three signs for "call" (summon, telephone, name) have been cross-indexed. The sign for "shout, scream" can also be used to mean "call". It is the teacher's responsibility to explain this aspect of manual communication.

Another new feature of the revised text is the use of parentheses to show that a variation of hand-shape and/or movement changes the word-equivalent of a sign, e.g. disagree, opposite, enemy. The text illustrates the sign for "opposite" with the words "disagree" and "enemy, opponent" in parenthesis. The instructor should teach the variations.

The author has tried to avoid the inclusion of "new" signs *per se*. In cases where initialized versions of certain signs—e.g. *c*lass, *g*roup, *o*rganization, etc. have become fairly wide-spread, they are included. Many experimenters, however, tend to go overboard and initialize everything. Unless the initialized sign is standard, or gaining widespread acceptance, do not expect to see it here. Of course, the teacher should be fully conversant with the various modes of manual communication and be prepared to explain to students *when* and *where* the use of such initialized signs is appropriate.

The revised edition of *A Basic Course in Manual Communication*, like the original text, owes much to all those books on manual communication that preceded it, especially Louie J. Fant, Jr's. *Say It with Hands*. Features of Fant's text continue to be incorporated herein, including the grouping of signs by the three basic parts: (1) the shape of the hands, (2) the place where the hands move to and from and (3) the movement (as described by Dr. William C. Stokoe, Jr. in *Sign Language Structure: An Outline of the Visual Communication Systems of the American Deaf*. Buffalo, New York: University of Buffalo, 1960).

And, last but not least, the author is indebted to all those teachers of Communicative Skills Program pilot classes whose feedback resulted in many of the changes incorporated in the new text.

MANUAL COMMUNICATION

The term *manual communication* is a broad one and encompasses five separate modes. In 1960 a monograph by William C. Stokoe, Jr. (*Sign Language Structure: An Outline of the Visual Communication Systems of the American Deaf* [Studies in Linguistics, Occasional Papers 8], Buffalo, New York) clearly defined the primary mode of manual communication—*sign language*. However, one must consider that *manual communication* in practice actually involves (1) *Sign Language*, (2) *Signed English*, (3) *Simultaneous Method*, (4) *Fingerspelling*, and (5) *Manual English*, which are used both in combination and separately.

The Linguistic Reporter, Vol. 12, No. 2, April 1970 carries a report of the "CAL Conference on Sign Languages" by William C. Stokoe, Jr. that elucidates on the five modes of manual communication which is quoted below:

> "Sign Language (1) is a language in which what are commonly called gestures do the usual work of words, or more precisely, in which cheremes (Stokoe, *Sign Language* ... p. 30ff.) are found instead of phonemes. But, most important, it is also a language that has its own morphology, syntax, and semantics. Dependence on or derivation from any spoken language has never been proven of the syntax, and semology of American Sign Language; and since the chereme-to-phoneme and the morpheme-to-morpheme relations of this language and English are demonstrably non-isomorphic, the independence of American Sign Language as a language can hardly be doubted.
>
> Most of what hearing observers see, including the interpretation witnessed by the conference participants, is not Sign Language, however, but Signed English (2). Using English syntax, this is a rapid succession of signs glossing the content words of an English utterance more or less approximately and glossing some function words, but not all. It usually includes fingerspelled words as well as signs. Both the signer and the addressee in this mode must know English well, because the signs are put together as if they were English words and not by the rules of Sign Language syntax. For example, the signs glossed 'perhaps, finish, be, forget', in that order, mean nothing in Sign Language but are produced and understood as the Signed English equivalent to *may have been forgotten*.
>
> In the Simultaneous Method (3) the speaker-signer conceives, encodes, and utters English at the same time he accompanies that utterance with Signed English. The deaf person as signer-speaker may speak, i.e. actually use his voice, or only mouth the words. As the addressee, he is able to use the speaker's facial movements as a check on the simultaneous manual production. Here, too, competence in English is essential, as is knowledge of the signs of sign language, but in the simultaneous mode a highly proficient user may make one of the channels explain the other. For example, American Sign Language has a sign glossed 'interview' or 'talk with', sometimes 'converse'; the participants of the conference noted that Mr. Pimentel said "conversant with" as he made that sign and then the sign 'with'. His noticeable slowing down at that point made clear to other users of the simultaneous mode that he was

expecting them to see that he was making the signs 'converse' and 'with' match the phrase "conversant with." Whereas the usual focus of contrastive studies is on negative interference of the languages a bilingual person speaks and thinks with, it seems here that the signer-speaker can use the unique relation of the simultaneous systems for mutual reinforcement.

Fingerspelling (4) is a system of making English utterances visible with hand positions and configurations for the twenty-six letters of the alphabet. For short stretches it can be sent and received rapidly enough to keep up with normal speaking, but long and constant practice is needed for such proficiency, and fingerspelling easily fatigues both sender and receiver when interchanges continue for long. Because, ideally it can present a one-to-one equivalence to the sequential alphabetical symbols of correctly spelled, idiomatic, and grammatical English structures, it has been advocated as a panacea for the educational problems arising from deafness, especially when used with speech and called "The Rochester Method." Most deaf persons prefer other modes but find fingerspelling indispensable and use it in Signed English as a supplement to signing in English order. Of course as a simple code for the symbols of writing it is trivial in any consideration of sign language.

Besides combining Signed English (2) and Fingerspelling (4) and these at times with speech (3), deaf persons and hearing teachers since the time of Epee have experimented with a more complete representation of a spoken language in signs. Manual English (5) augments the signs that translate the semantic component of English words with signs invented to represent some of the more important functional morphemes. Thus, in Hoemann's manual (Harry W. Hoemann [ed.], *Improved Techniques of Communication: A Training Manual for Use with Severely Handicapped Deaf Clients* [Bowling Green, Ohio: Psychology Department, Bowling Green State University, 1970) there are signs for the plural, past tense, present participial, and infinitive morphemes, and for many derivational suffixes. These are signed in English (surface) order, of course, so that the signing takes on a more nearly morpheme-by-morpheme equivalence to English. This way of encoding English is not trivial, because it is based on certain assumptions about the lexicons of English and American Sign Language which involve whole morphological and semantic systems. Already the advocates of a signed representation of English morphemes have had to make arbitrary choices: *cowboy* is signed 'cow' and 'boy', but *understand* is not signed 'under' and 'stand' (though making the sign 'stand' upside down for 'understand' is still a good bilingual pun). A complete sign-morpheme treatment of English, could it be achieved, would constitute an entirely new sign language. Concessions like that of using a single sign for *understand*, *butterfly*, and *overcome* reveal that American Sign Language already has its own inventory of morphemes and that its semantic system is tied to them and not to the English word stock."

It is important that the student of *manual communication* understand these differences. *Sign Language* is basically concept-oriented, that is, gestures do the work of words but do not have a gesture-word relationship, rather a gesture-concept relationship.

The average prelingually deaf person uses concept-related signs and a syntax that is unrelated to English. The sign for *ability* (#516), for example, expresses the concept of *expertise*. Thus it would be used in such sentences as: "He is a *skilled* electrician"; "He has the *ability* to do the job"; "He is a baseball *expert*."

Such signs as "potato" (#601) and "infirmary" (#614) have what approximates a gesture-word relationship. The development of a new and expanded vocabulary of signs as in Bornstein, Hamilton, and Kannapell, *Signs for Instructional Purposes*. Washington, D.C.: Gallaudet College Press, 1969, has attempted to come up with a gesture-word relationship. Many of the "new" signs however (such as "theory" (p. 17)) are simply initializations of the basic signs. It would thus follow that a knowledge of the basic signs is essential *prior to* learning any of the more sophisticated modes of manual communication.

Most hearing individuals who are learning *manual communication* tend to adapt signs to *Signed English*. That is, they use a combination of English syntax (and oftentimes speech, which then becomes the Simultaneous Method) and signs. For expressive purposes, especially in the educational setting, this would probably be considered a preferred mode. However, when on the receiving end of a conversation with the average prelingually deaf person who uses Sign Language they are often at a complete loss.

No one can expect to master a language overnight. It has been said that it takes four or five years to master a language and even then, the individual will not have the skill of a native speaker. One can, however, spend three months studying the language of some primeval tribe and earn a Ph.D. in Linguistics for describing it.

The above is not to say that learning manual communication is especially difficult. One who wishes to learn, however, must avail himself of all opportunities *to use* the new skill he is acquiring. The more opportunity the student has to associate with deaf individuals, especially those of a varied educational background, the more he will learn not only of the various modes of manual communication, but of the particular settings in which they are used. Too much stress cannot be put on providing a practicuum for students of manual communication which will provide them with many and varied experiences for reinforcement and additional learning.

It should be pointed out that there are local, state, and regional differences in signs. The signs included in this text have been chosen on the basis of "most frequent usage" but are not intended to be *the* signs.

A teacher should never arbitrarily say that such and such a sign is correct or incorrect; rather it should be explained that one sign may be correct in Texas, but not in Maine; or one sign may be correct in colloquial conversation, but not on the speaker's podium. Just as there are differences in the pronunciation of English words in different regions, and the choice of a specific English word in a specific situation is highly dependent on the speaker's educational, cultural, and environmental experience, the choice of a specific sign or mode of manual communication is likewise dependent on the experience of the speaker. An understanding of this facilitates communication, be it manual or spoken.

Another aspect of manual communication that must be elucidated by the teacher is the use of facial expression and other body movements. One does not, for example, smile when he gives the sign for "cross, irritated" (#151), but rather makes an angry frown. This use of "body English" might be equated with *inflection* in the human voice.

No book, however, could begin to "teach" this aspect of manual communication and, again exposure to deaf individuals who use this form of communication is of primary importance.

For excellent description of the paralinguistic nuances and subtleties of sign language the student could be referred to Falberg, Roger M., *The Language of Silence* (see "Manual Communication Bibliography," p. 122, and "A Selected Annotated Bibliography of Books, Films, and Teaching Media on Sign Language," p. 131).

LESSON 1
FINGER SPELLING

The excerpts below are taken from the supplemental text that is suggested for use by all students.

Reprinted from EXPRESSIVE AND RECEPTIVE FINGERSPELLING FOR HEARING ADULTS by La Vera M. Guillory. Published by Claitor's Publishing Division, Baton Rouge, Louisiana.

Since this material was developed specifically for teaching adult hearing persons to fingerspell, it is taken for granted that the adult hears, speaks and also has fully developed reading and writing skills. However, it might be of interest to know that during its origin the method was experimentally used to teach an illiterate, seventy-year-old person, who in ten or fifteen minutes, learned to fingerspell and recognize several words in the *an, can, ran* series.

An old and common approach to fingerspelling was that the interested hearing person obtained a manual alphabet card, from which he learned the twenty-six different hand positions that represent the letters of the alphabet. Then he set about spelling out words letter by letter.

With constant practice this person eventually learned to spell and see words, but, in many instances, others using this method continued to spell out each word and to see only letters, *never whole words*, when reading fingerspelling. Even after becoming quite skilled in the action of forming the letters and in recognizing those letters they saw, many apparently either did not realize they were expected to see words or if they did, failed to break the old habit of spelling and reading letter by letter.

The hearing "letter-reading" teacher must be a source of constant frustration to the deaf pupil, especially to the older pupil who has a large vocabulary. What emotional strain must be experienced when a pupil, required to give answers in fingerspelling, must spell each letter individually in order that the teacher can recognize each letter of each word! To analogize, the situation might be comparable to a hearing person forced to spell letter by letter instead of speaking words, to a skilled typist forced to type letter by letter, or someone accustomed to write as fast as he can think forced to decrease his speed to a slow, deliberate pace, carefully forming each letter of every word. Another analogy is a class with the hearing teacher spelling to her hearing pupils, and they, in turn, spelling every answer or thought expressed in a class discussion.

Two factors in fingerspelling are quite obvious—first, the physical actions of expressing an idea and second, the visual action of receiving one. In using the Rochester Method, a third factor is involved. We must be constantly aware that the fingerspelling is used only to supplement speech and lipreading. Therefore, we must speak or silently form every word on the lips at the same instant it is spelled. The phonetic sound necessary for lipreading must appear on the lips and the hand at the same instant.

The first rule of fingerspelling and speaking words simultaneously might be *to let the fingers set the pace for speech*. To do this, it is necessary to form the habit of thinking longer words in syllables.

THE USE OF PHONETIC COMBINATIONS

The configurations shown on the succeeding pages were designed to be used in learning the basic phonetic elements of words. For their utilization, one must understand that they are to be used for the development of the ability to fingerspell words.

For illustration, take the word *an*. In writing this word with pen or pencil, one would think *an*, not the individual letters, *a-n*. In fingerspelling, one should be trained to follow the same method of thinking the whole word *an*, as the letters *a-n* are formed on the hand. After it has become automatic to think the word while spelling out the letters, one can precede *an* by the letter *b*. The formation becomes *b-a-n*, but the thought must be *ban*. When the word *ban* becomes routine, a new word can be formed by substituting the letter *c* for the *b* to form the word *can*. The same procedure can be followed through the family of words — *fan, man, pan, ran, tan, van.*

After the first family of words has been mastered, it becomes successively easier to master the others.

Much concentration and practice plus determination and a true desire to learn will speed the learning process. Who could have more motivation for learning than a hearing person vitally interested in the deaf? It is a physical impossibility for some deaf persons to learn to speak our language perfectly. We must learn to use their medium.

BASIC PHONETIC ELEMENTS IN THREE-LETTER RHYMING WORDS

ab

ad

ag

am

an

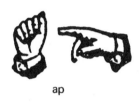

ap

ar

as

at

ay

ax

LESSON 2
NUMBERS

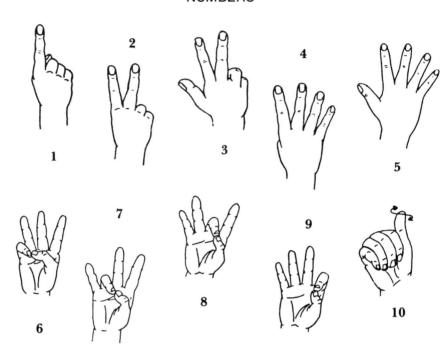

His new phone number is ten times easier. Just dial area code 987/654-3210.

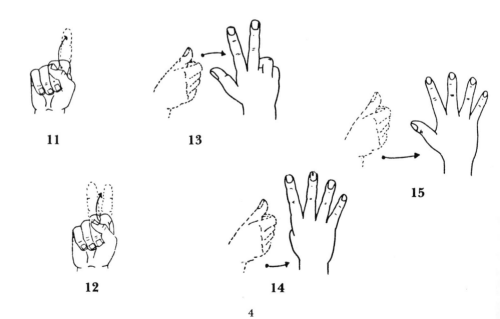

4

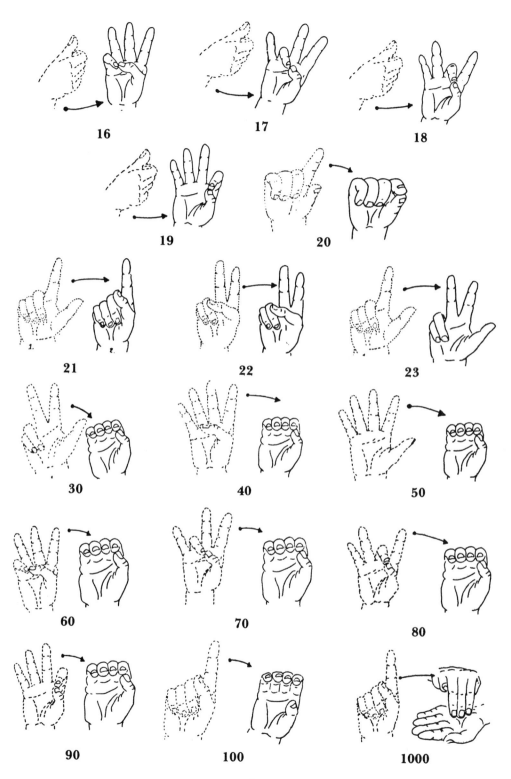

16

17

18

19

20

21

22

23

30

40

50

60

70

80

90

100

1000

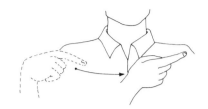

LESSON 3

WE (See also: 676) 4

1

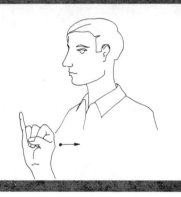

US 5

ME 2

MY, MINE 6

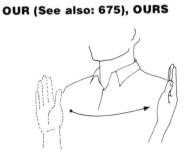

YOU (singular),
(YOU (plural)) 3

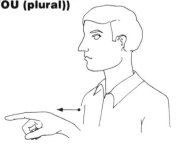

OUR (See also: 675), OURS 7

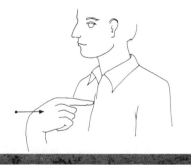

YOUR, YOURS (singular), (YOURS (plural)) 8

MYSELF 9

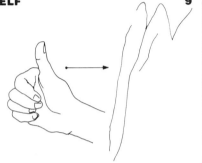

YOURSELVES, (YOURSELF) 10

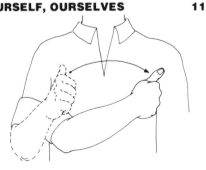

OURSELF, OURSELVES 11

WHO, WHOM, WHOSE 12

LESSON 4

BECAUSE, SINCE 13
(See also: 103)

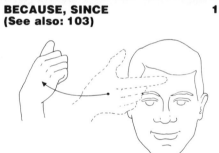

IN, INSIDE 14

OUT, OUTSIDE 15

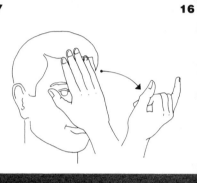

WHY 16

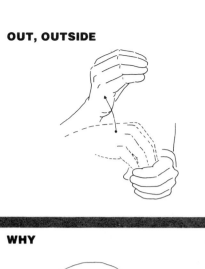

ON 17

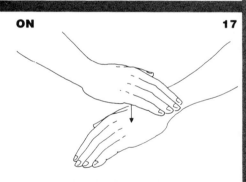

FOR 18

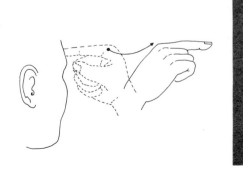

TOGETHER, ACCOMPANY 19

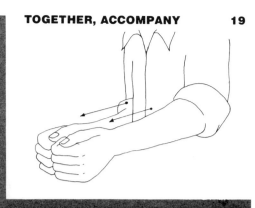

WITH 20

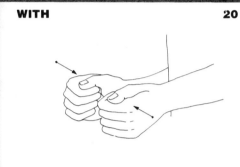

WITHOUT 21

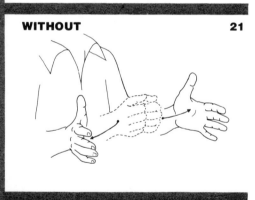

THAT (See also: 715) 22

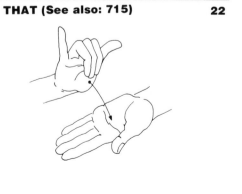

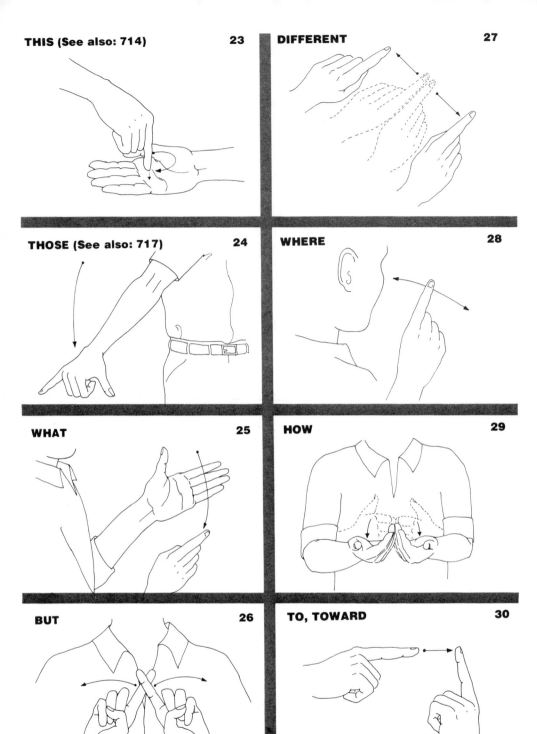

THIS (See also: 714) 23

DIFFERENT 27

THOSE (See also: 717) 24

WHERE 28

WHAT 25

HOW 29

BUT 26

TO, TOWARD 30

UNTIL 31

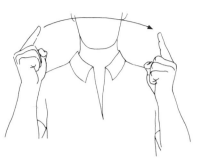

ABOVE 35

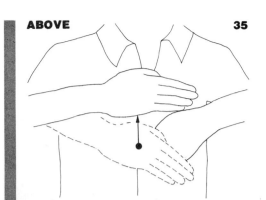

WHEN 32

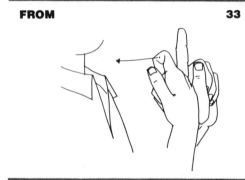

BELOW 36

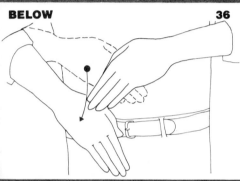

FROM 33

ENTER, INTO 37

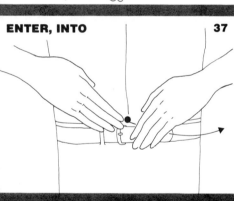

UNDER, BENEATH, (BASEMENT) 34

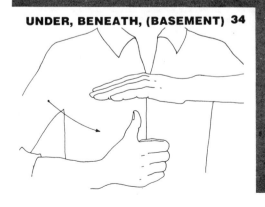

LESSON 5

NONE, NO (quantitative no)   41

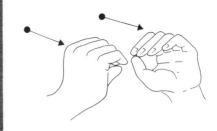

WON'T, WOULDN'T, REFUSE   38

NO   42

CAN'T, COULDN'T IMPOSSIBLE (DM)   39

NOT, DON'T, DOESN'T, ISN'T   43

NOTHING   40

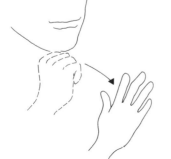

NOT, DON'T, DOESN'T, ISN'T, (DENY)   44

NEVER 45

CLEAN, NICE, (CLEANING (DM), CLEAN UP (DM)) 48

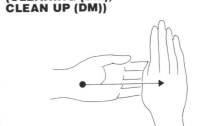

LESSON 6

SCHOOL 49

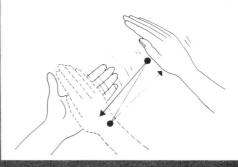

ACROSS, OVER (See also: 730) 46

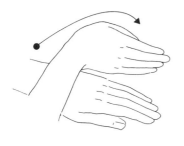

COLLEGE, (UNIVERSITY) 50

NOW 47

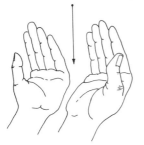

PERHAPS, MAYBE, PROBABLY 51

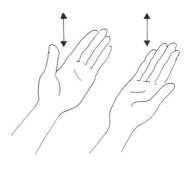

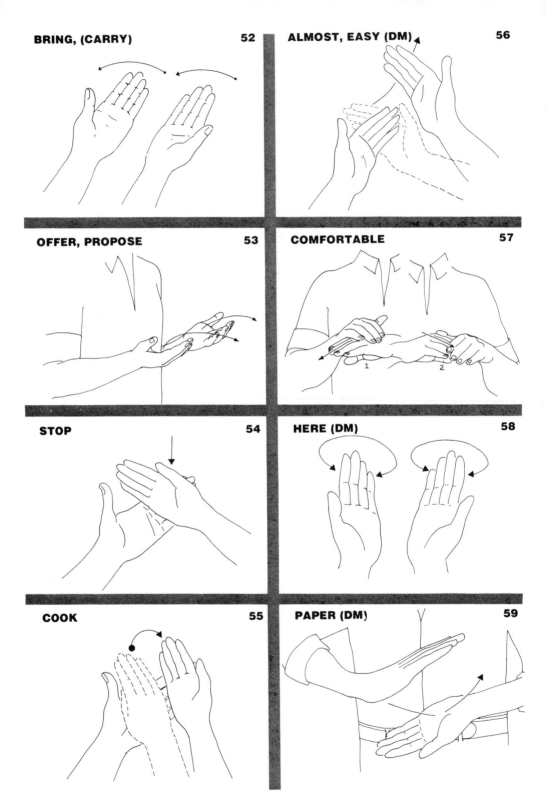

BRING, (CARRY)   52

ALMOST, EASY (DM)   56

OFFER, PROPOSE   53

COMFORTABLE   57

STOP   54

HERE (DM)   58

COOK   55

PAPER (DM)   59

14

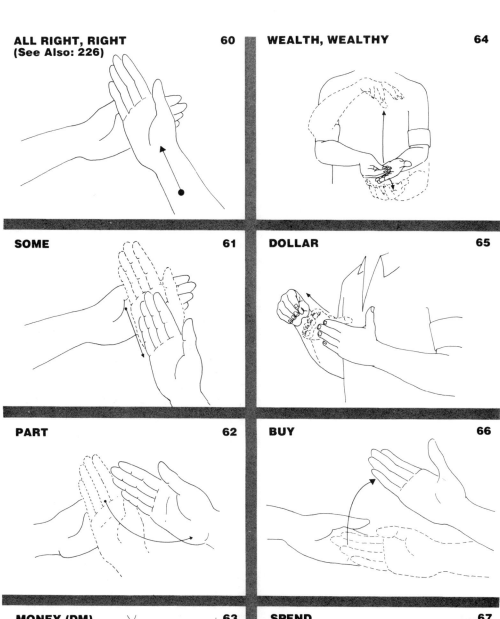

ALL RIGHT, RIGHT 60
(See Also: 226)

SOME 61

PART 62

MONEY (DM) 63

WEALTH, WEALTHY 64

DOLLAR 65

BUY 66

SPEND 67

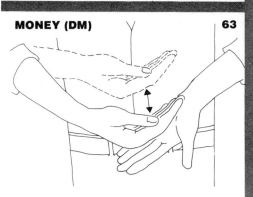
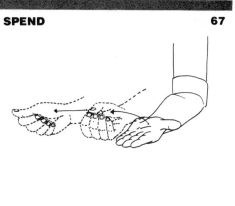

CHEAP 68

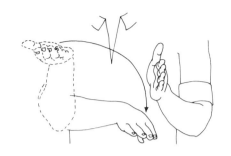

LESSON, CHAPTER, COURSE 72

EXPENSIVE 69

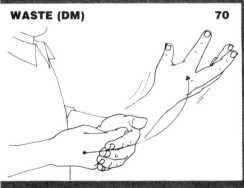

PARDON, EXCUSE, FORGIVE, 73
(DISMISS, LAY OFF)

WASTE (DM) 70

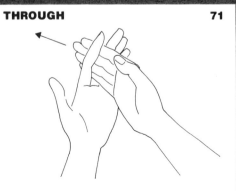

NEW 74

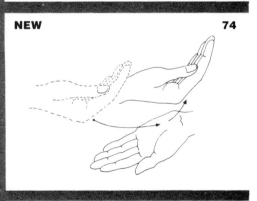

THROUGH 71

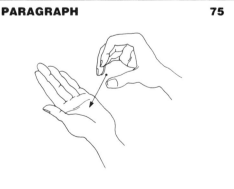

PARAGRAPH 75

LIST (noun) 76

LESSON 7

LIST (verb) 77

THINK 79

FISH 78

THINKING, WONDERING, (REASON) 80

LONG 81

17

HEAR 82

UNDERSTAND 86

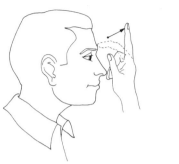

ALWAYS 83

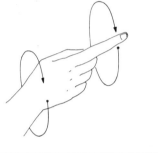

INTELLIGENT, BRILLIANT 87

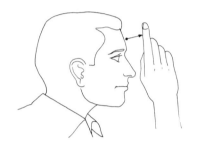

ONLY 84

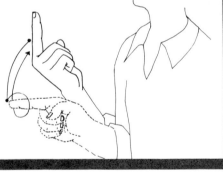

BLACK 88

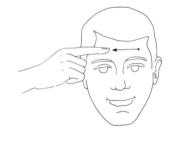

FACE, LOOKS
(personal appearance) 85

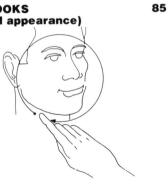

LESSON 8

TOMORROW 92

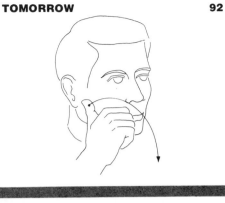

MEMORIZE 89

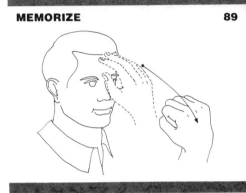

YESTERDAY 93

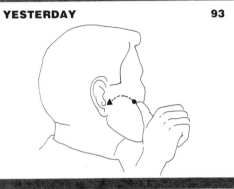

EVERYDAY, DAILY 90

SORRY 94

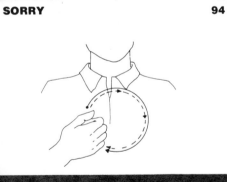

ANOTHER, OTHER, ELSE 91
(See also: 737)

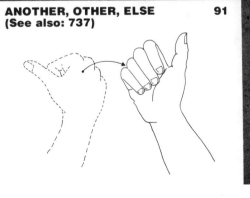

PRIDE 95

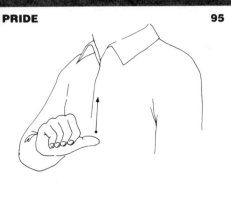

OPERATION, SURGERY 96

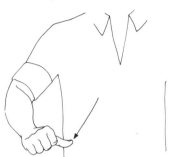

ANY 97

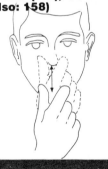

HANDKERCHIEF (DM), COLD (DM) (See also: 158) 98

CANADA 99

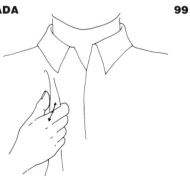

SECRET 100

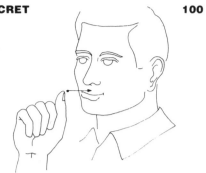

PATIENCE, BEAR, ENDURE, (SUFFER) 101

LESSON 9

DURING, WHILE 102

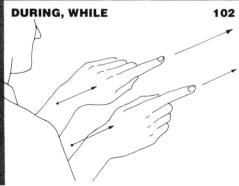

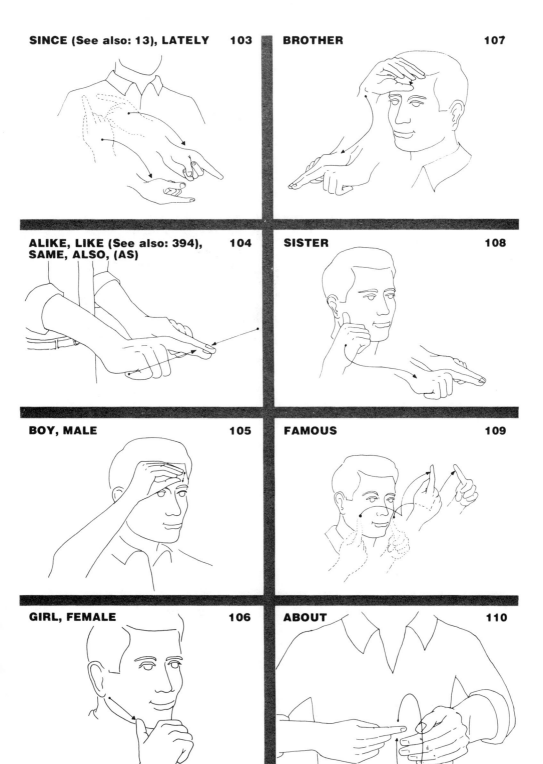

SINCE (See also: 13), LATELY   103

BROTHER   107

ALIKE, LIKE (See also: 394), SAME, ALSO, (AS)   104

SISTER   108

BOY, MALE   105

FAMOUS   109

GIRL, FEMALE   106

ABOUT   110

AROUND 111

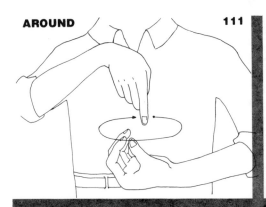

ANSWER 115

SIGN (See also: 500) 112

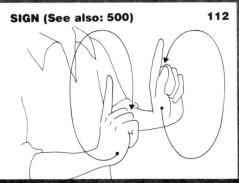

LESSON 10

COME 113

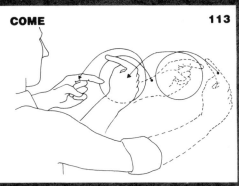

WASH 116

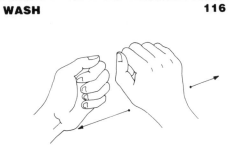

GO 114

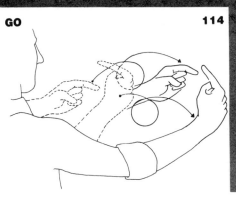

BATH, BATHE 117

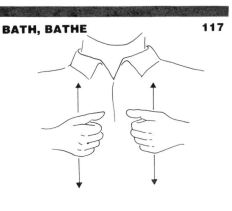

22

REMEMBER, MEMORY (DM) 118

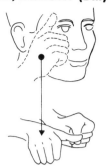

ASSOCIATE, MINGLE, EACH OTHER 122

LIVE, RESIDENCE, ADDRESS 119

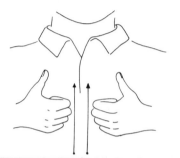

DRAMA, PLAY
(See also: 650), ACT 123

LIFE 120

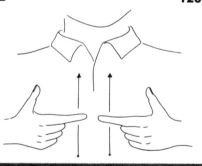

AMBITION 124

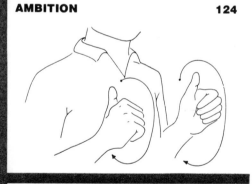

SWEETHEART 121

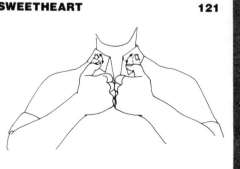

CARDS, DEAL 125

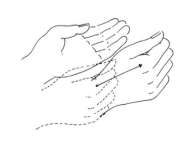

23

FOLLOW, (CHASE), (AVOID), (CATCH UP) 126

WHETHER (See also: 736), WHICH 130

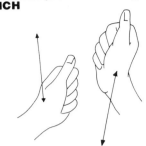

PASS 127

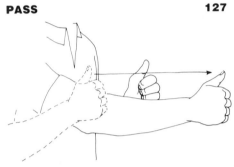

SUBSTITUTE, EXCHANGE, TRADE 131

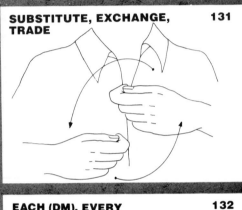

MOST, —EST (See also: 686) 128

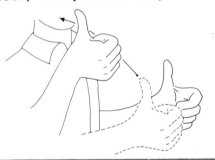

EACH (DM), EVERY 132

COAT 129

SCIENCE 133

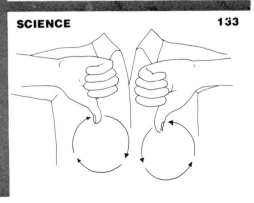

LESSON 11

WARM 137

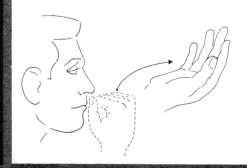

POLITE 134

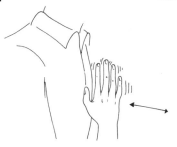

MOTHER 138

FINE 135

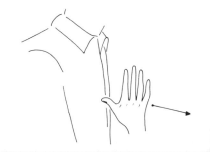

GRANDMOTHER 139

HOT 136

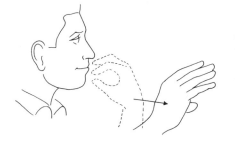

FATHER 140

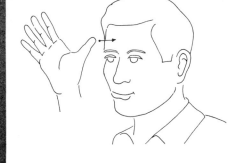

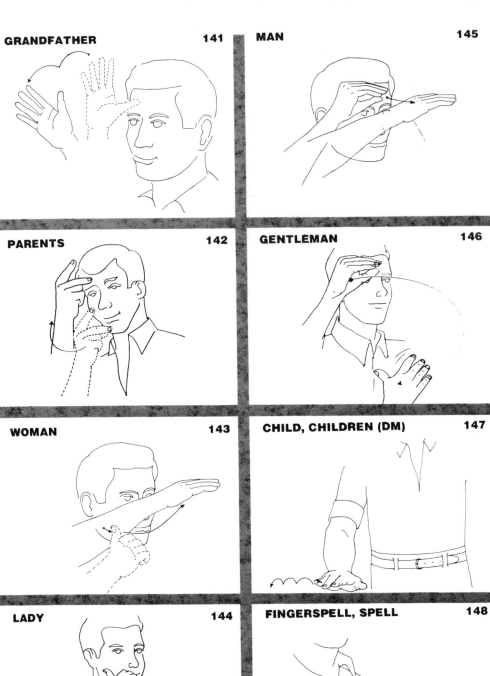

GRANDFATHER 141

MAN 145

PARENTS 142

GENTLEMAN 146

WOMAN 143

CHILD, CHILDREN (DM) 147

LADY 144

FINGERSPELL, SPELL 148

COLOR 149

LESSON 12

COMPLAIN, GRIPE 150

SHOES 152

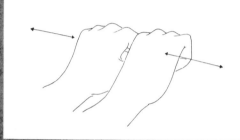

CROSS, IRRITATED 151

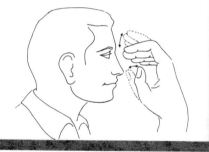

CUSTOM, HABIT 153

ATTEMPT, TRY, EFFORT 154

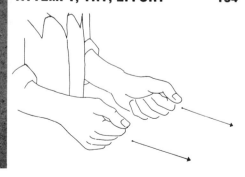

MAY, CAN, ABLE, POSSIBLE (DM)   155

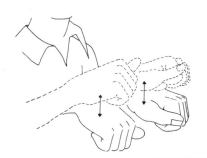

EXERCISE   159

BREAK   156

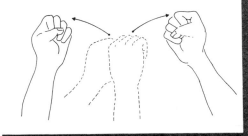

CAR, DRIVE   160

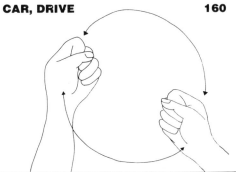

DOUBT   157

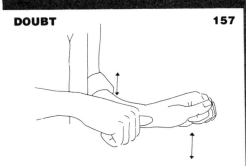

WORK   161

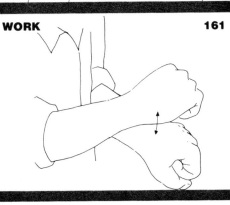

COLD, (See also: 98), WINTER   158

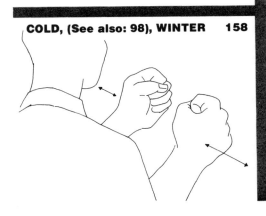

LESSON 13

NERVOUS   165

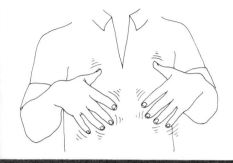

SAD   162

AMERICA   166

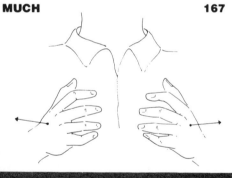

FIRE, (See also: 339), BURN   163

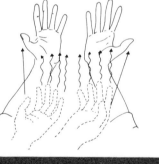

MUCH   167

BASKETBALL   164

SHOWER (DM)   168

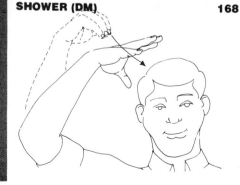

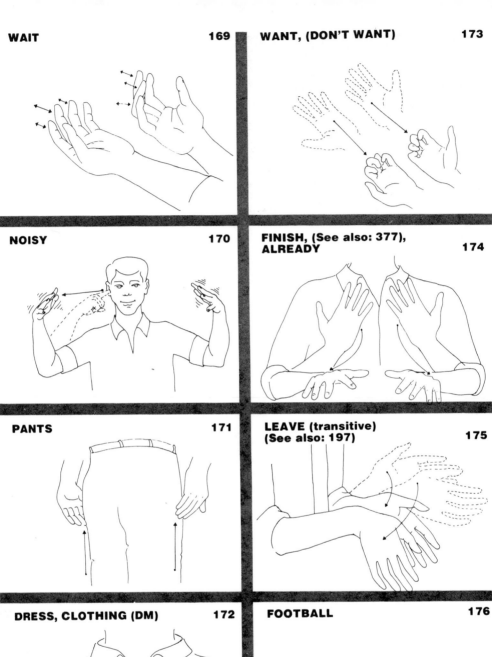

WAIT   169

WANT, (DON'T WANT)   173

NOISY   170

FINISH, (See also: 377), ALREADY   174

PANTS   171

LEAVE (transitive) (See also: 197)   175

DRESS, CLOTHING (DM)   172

FOOTBALL   176

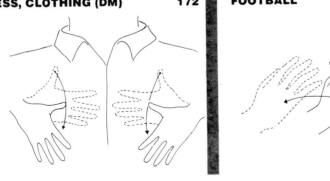

FRIGHTEN, SCARE, AFRAID 177

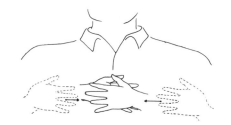

FEAR 178

LESSON 14

OPEN 179

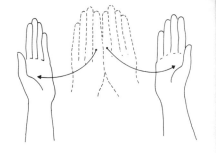

CLOSE 180

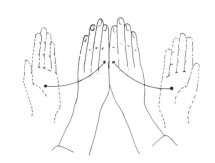

BOOK 181

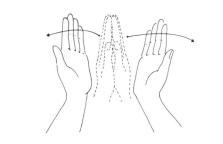

DAY 182

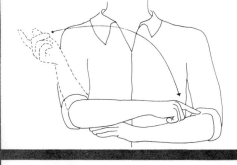

MORNING 183

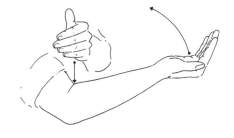

NOON   184

ASK (See also: 631), REQUEST, (PRAY (DM))   188

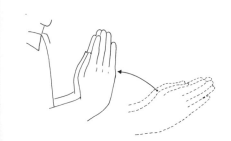

AFTERNOON   185

ENTHUSIASTIC (DM)   189

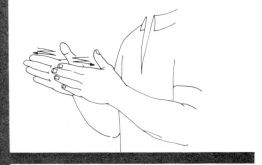

NIGHT   186

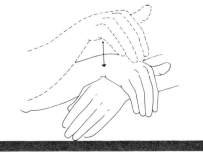

TABLE, DESK   190

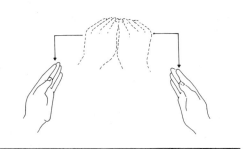

ALL NIGHT, OVERNIGHT   187

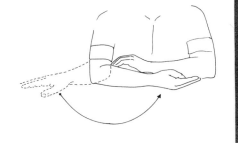

AGAIN, REPEAT (DM)   191

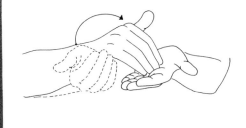

OFTEN 192

ALL, WHOLE 193

INCLUDE, INVOLVE 194

MORE 195

ANYWAY, REGARDLESS, IT DOESN'T MATTER 196

LEAVE (See also: 175), DEPART 197

COMPARE 198

LOSE 199

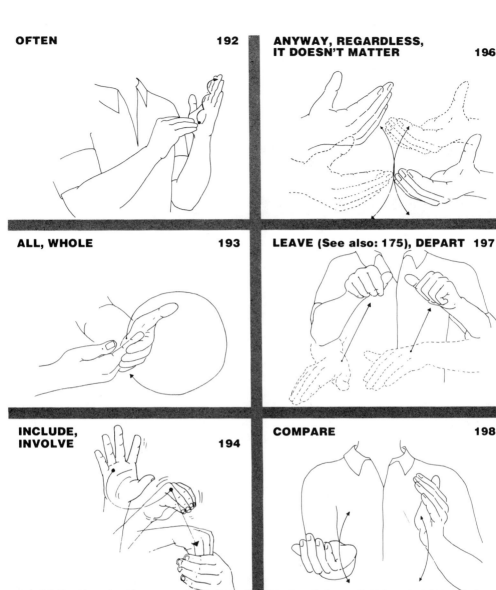

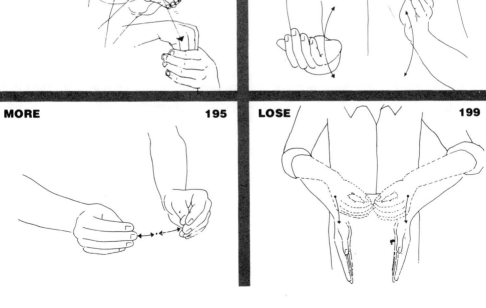

33

LESSON 15

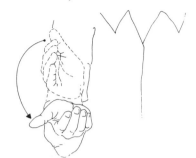

LECTURE, SPEECH 200
(See also: 216), (PREACH)

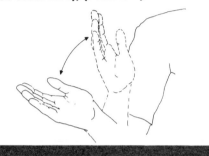

BEFORE 204

FUTURE, WILL, SHALL 201

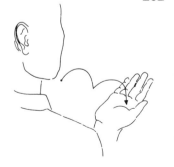

PAST, LAST, (See also: 423), 205
AGO, FORMERLY, PREVIOUSLY

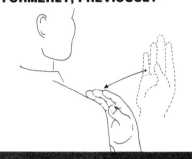

THING 202

KNOW, (DON'T KNOW) 206

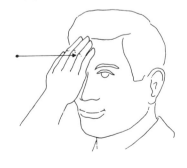

34

LESSON 16

CARELESS (DM) 210

SEE 207

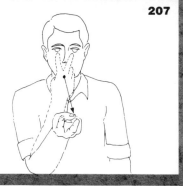

VOICE 211

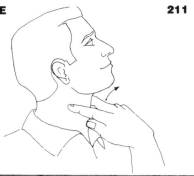

BLIND 208

LIPREAD, ORAL (school) 212

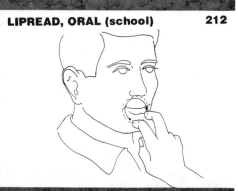

LOOK AT, WATCH 209

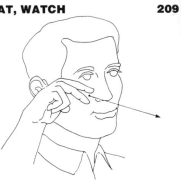

IGNORANT, STUPID 213

35

MISUNDERSTAND 214

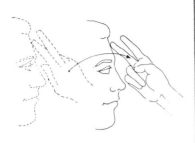

TELL 217

STEAL 215

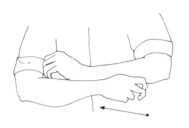

ANNOUNCE 218

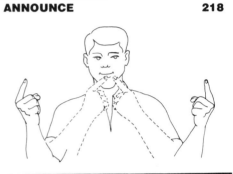

LESSON 17

TRUE, REAL, SURE 219

SPEECH (See also: 200), SAY, SAID, SPOKE, TALK (See also: 232) 216

LONELY 220

ALONE	**221**	**SMILE, LAUGH (DM)**	**225**

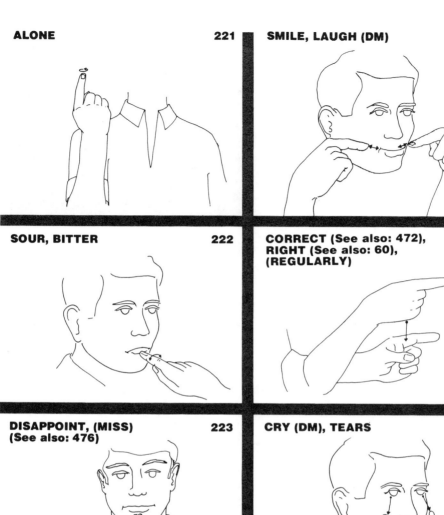

SOUR, BITTER   **222**

CORRECT (See also: 472), RIGHT (See also: 60), (REGULARLY)   **226**

DISAPPOINT, (MISS)   **223**
(See also: 476)

CRY (DM), TEARS   **227**

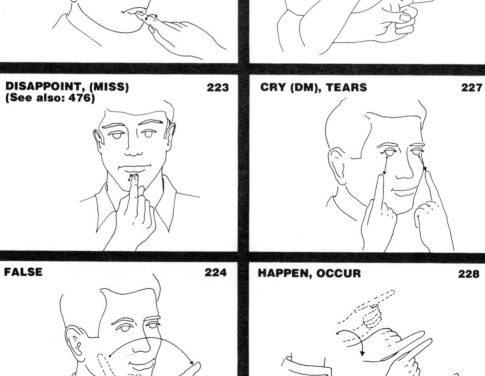

FALSE   **224**

HAPPEN, OCCUR   **228**

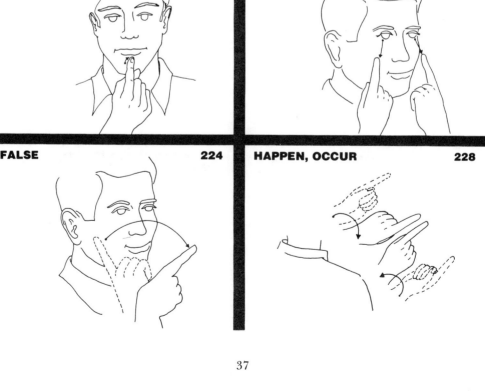

37

MEET (a person) (See also: 333) 229

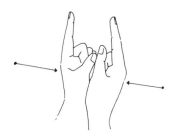

LESSON 18

SUCCEED 230

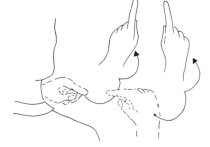

PRETTY, (BEAUTIFUL) 233

AGREE 231

FLOWER 234

TALK (See also: 216), CONVERSE 232

EAT, FOOD, (BREAKFAST), (LUNCH), (DINNER, SUPPER)

EXPERIENCE (DM) 236

FEW, A FEW, SEVERAL 240

SLEEP, SLEEPY (DM) 237

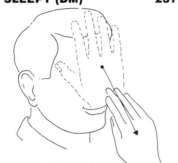

HOME 241

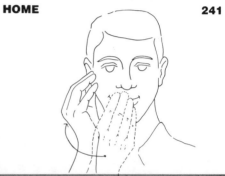

WHITE 238

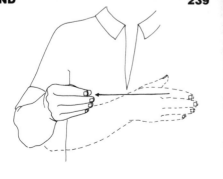

LESSON 19

AND 239

SELL, STORE (noun) (DM) 242

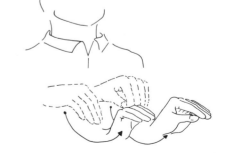

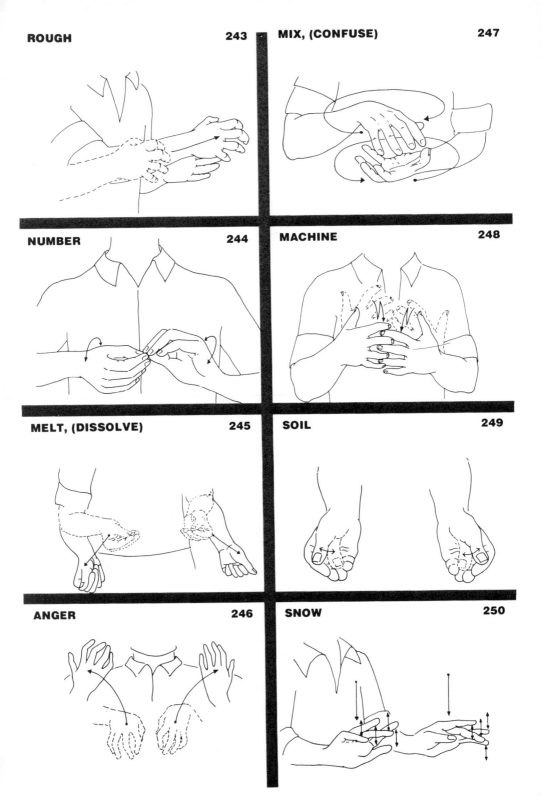

ROUGH 243

MIX, (CONFUSE) 247

NUMBER 244

MACHINE 248

MELT, (DISSOLVE) 245

SOIL 249

ANGER 246

SNOW 250

RAIN 251

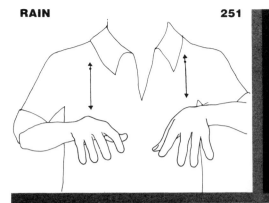

LESSON 20

MOVE, (PLACE (See also: 433)), (PUT) 252

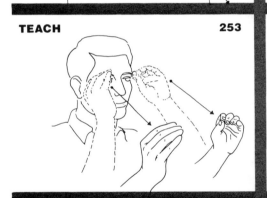

TEACH 253

HAPPY 254

PLEASURE, ENJOY, (PLEASE) 255

SUGAR (DM), CANDY (DM), (CUTE (DM)) 256

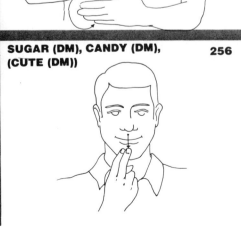

SWEET 257

SMELL (DM) 261

BAD 258

ASHAMED, (SHY) 262

GOOD 259

BREAD 263

THANK YOU 260

42

LESSON 21

MONDAY, TUESDAY, etc. 267

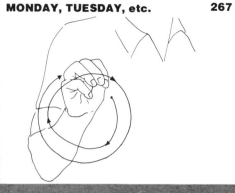

JAIL, PRISON 264

HAVE (possess) 268

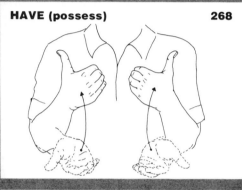

WONDERFUL 265

ANIMAL 269

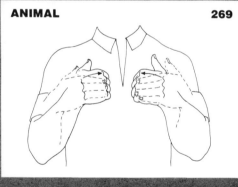

SUNDAY 266

AFTER 270

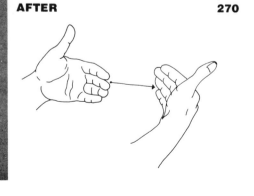

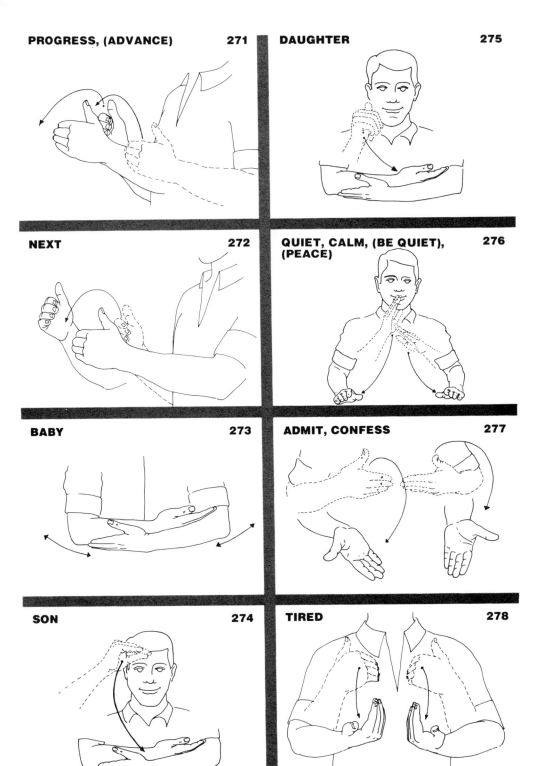

PROGRESS, (ADVANCE) 271

NEXT 272

BABY 273

SON 274

DAUGHTER 275

QUIET, CALM, (BE QUIET), (PEACE) 276

ADMIT, CONFESS 277

TIRED 278

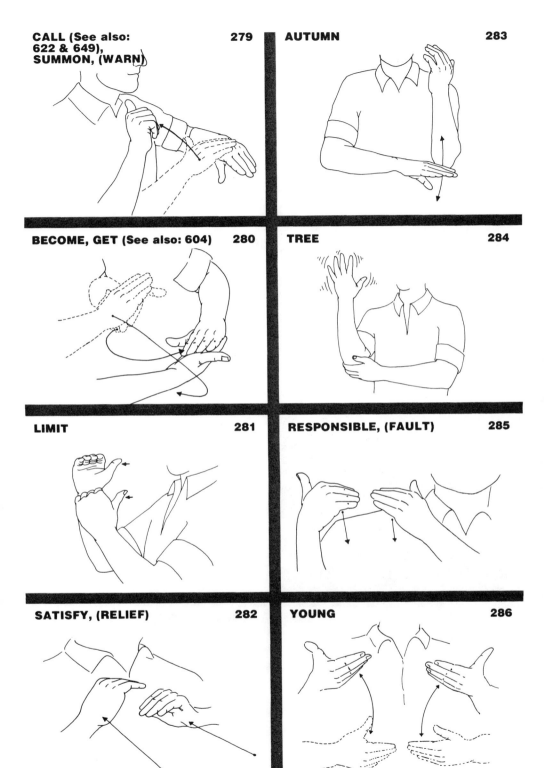

CALL (See also: 622 & 649), SUMMON, (WARN)   279

AUTUMN   283

BECOME, GET (See also: 604)   280

TREE   284

LIMIT   281

RESPONSIBLE, (FAULT)   285

SATISFY, (RELIEF)   282

YOUNG   286

45

BODY 287

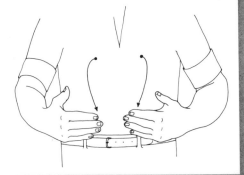

BEAT, DEFEAT 290

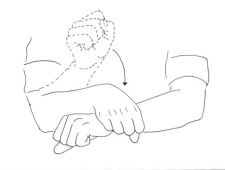

LIGHT (wt.), (See also: 330) 288

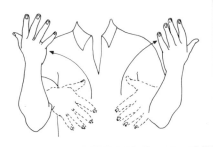

APPOINTMENT, RESERVATION 291

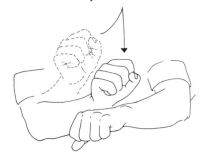

LESSON 22

BASEBALL 292

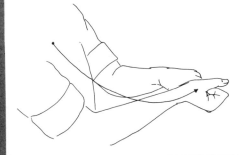

LOVE 289

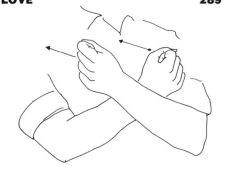

GUARD, PROTECT, DEFEND 293

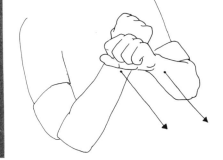

LIBERTY, FREE, SAVE (See also: 310)   294

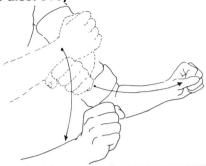

MAKE   298

YEAR   295

EXAGGERATE, (ADVERTISE (DM), PROPAGANDA (DM))

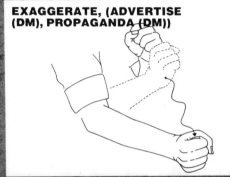

NEXT YEAR, (YEARLY)   296

LESSON 23

COFFEE   297

VISIT   300

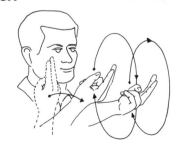

47

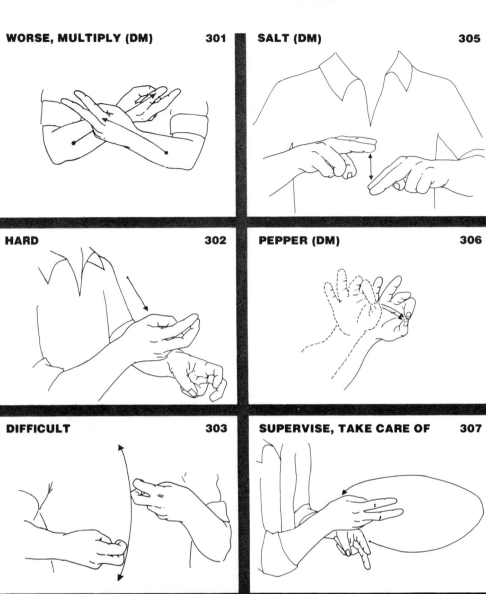

WORSE, MULTIPLY (DM) 301

HARD 302

DIFFICULT 303

SALT (DM) 305

PEPPER (DM) 306

SUPERVISE, TAKE CARE OF 307

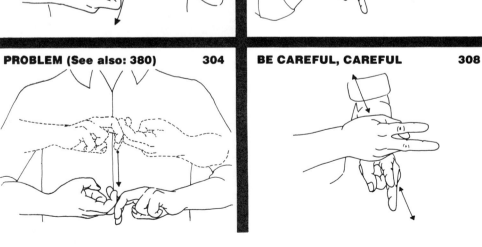

PROBLEM (See also: 380) 304

BE CAREFUL, CAREFUL 308

KEEP 309

SAVE (store away) (DM) 310
(See also: 294)

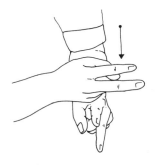

TRAIN (noun) (See also: 513) 311

BORROW, (LOAN) 312

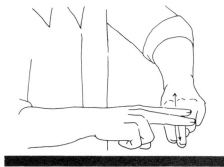

VERY 313

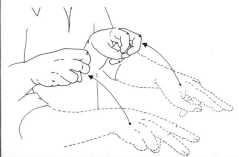

SELFISH 314

LESSON 24

GOAL, OBJECTIVE 315

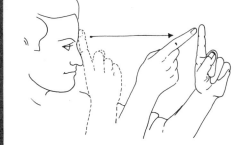

49

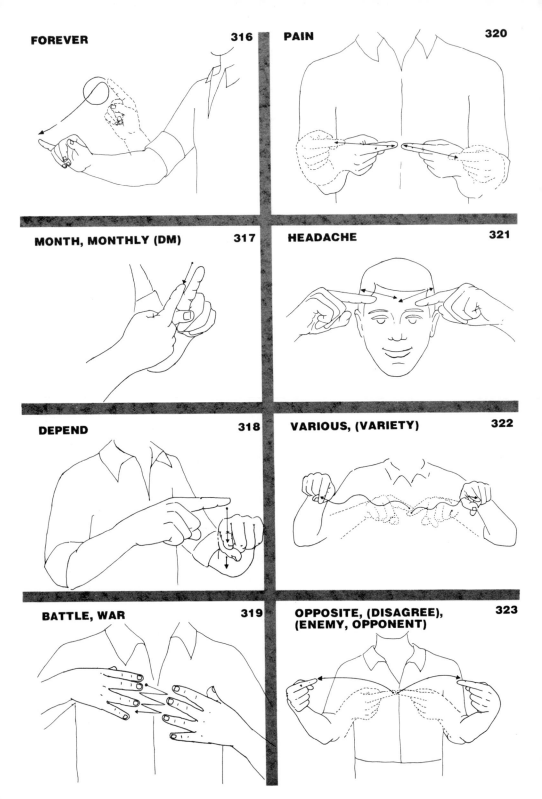

FOREVER 316

MONTH, MONTHLY (DM) 317

DEPEND 318

BATTLE, WAR 319

PAIN 320

HEADACHE 321

VARIOUS, (VARIETY) 322

OPPOSITE, (DISAGREE), (ENEMY, OPPONENT) 323

STRUGGLE 324

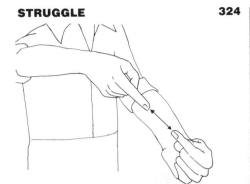

ARGUE (DM) (See also: 471), 325
(QUARREL (DM))

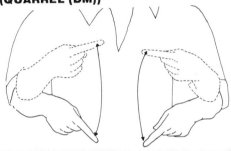

LESSON 25

OBEY, (NOTIFY, INFORM), 326
(INFORMATION)

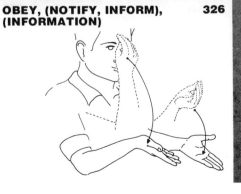

SOFT (DM) 327

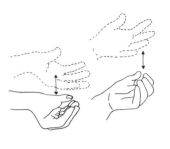

WET 328

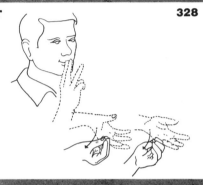

POOR 329

OBVIOUS, BRIGHT, CLEAR, 330
LIGHT (See also: 288)

ACCEPT 331

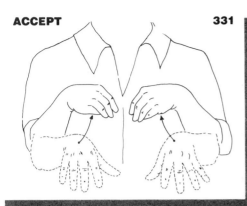

GIVE 332

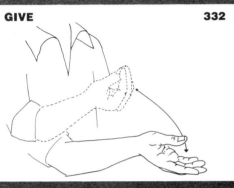

DEATH, DEAD 335

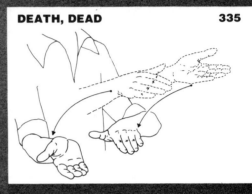

MEET (See also: 229), CONGREGATE, MEETING (DM) 333

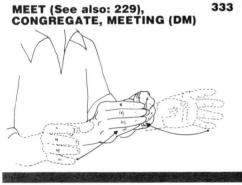

DARK 336

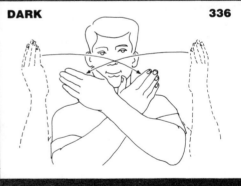

DESTROY, (MEAN) (See also: 565) 334

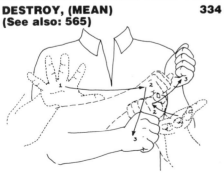

THAN 337

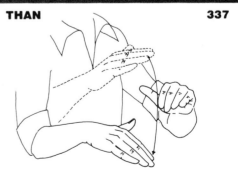

LESSON 26

52

SEND 338

FIRE (lose one's job) 339
(See also: 163)

SEPARATE 340

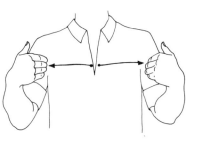

PLAN, ARRANGE, PREPARE 341

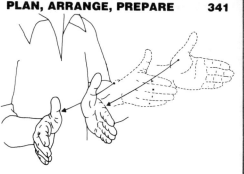

BOAT 342

ROAD, (RIVER), (OCEAN) 343

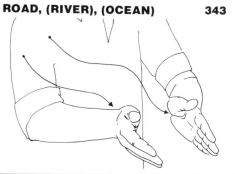

METHOD, WAY, STREET, PATH 344

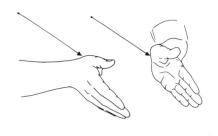

NARROW 345

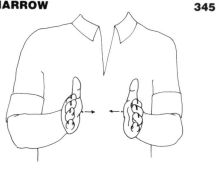

WIDE   346

HOUSE   350

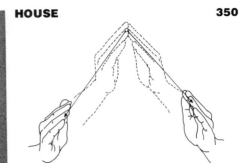

BORN, BIRTH   347

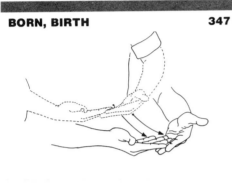

CITY, TOWN, COMMUNITY   351

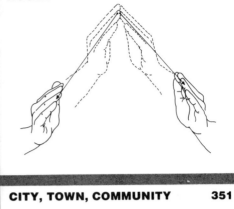

ALLOW, LET   348

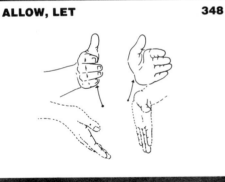

BUILD, BUILDING
(build + house)   352

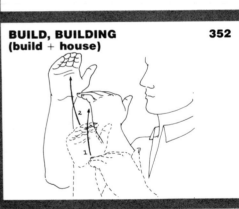

BASIC   349

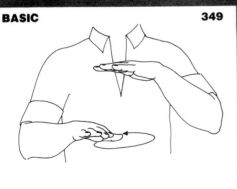

RUSSIA, RUSSIAN   353

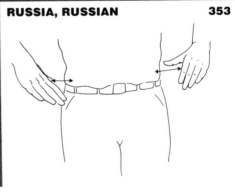

INTRODUCE 354

INVITE, WELCOME 355

MIRROR 356

WINDOW 357

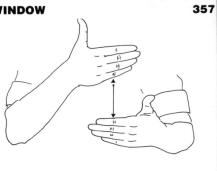

BOX, ROOM 358

DOOR 359

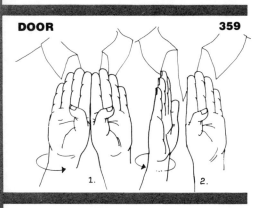

1.   2.

LATE, NOT YET 360

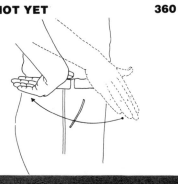

TOO MUCH, EXCESS 361

LESSON 27

ARRIVE, (CLOSE TO), (APPROACH) 365

HEAVY (wt.) 362

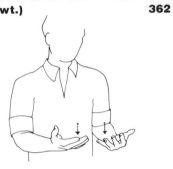

PROOF 366

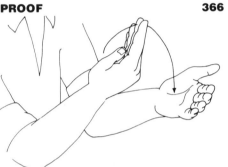

EQUAL 363

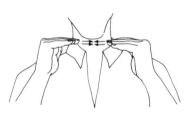

NEAR, (NEIGHBOR) 367

LESS, DECREASE 364

BETWEEN 368

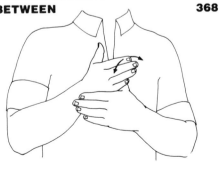

BESIDE 369

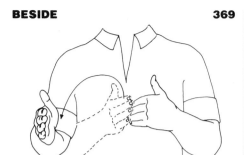

POWER, STRONG, (BRAVE) 373

BOTHER (DM) 370

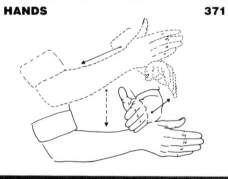

SLOW 374

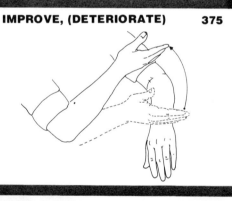

HANDS 371

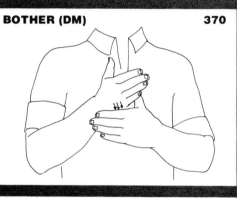

IMPROVE, (DETERIORATE) 375

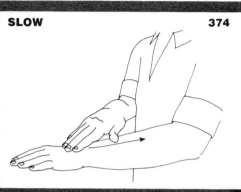

ENCOURAGE (DM) 372

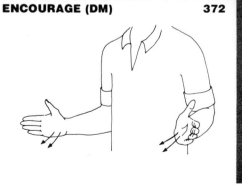

HIGH, (LOW) 376

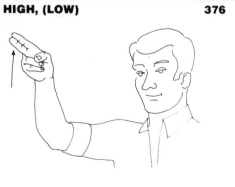

FINISH (See also: 174), END, COMPLETED, RESULT   **377**

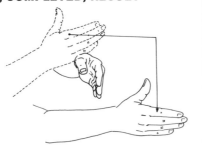

ATTENTION, CONCENTRATE   **381**

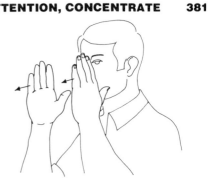

KIND   **378**

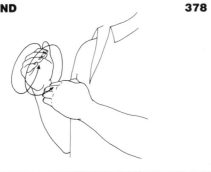

EMBARRASS, BLUSH   **382**

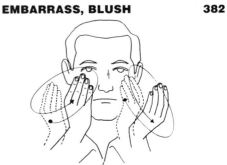

REST   **379**

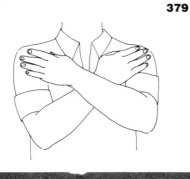

HEAD   **383**

WORRY, TROUBLE, PROBLEM   **380**
(See also: 304)

CENTER, MIDDLE   **384**

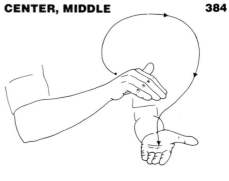

DIVIDE 385

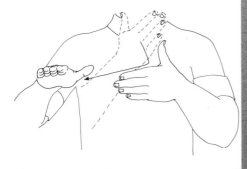

CAUSE 386

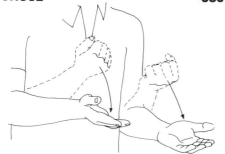

LESSON 28

SICK 387

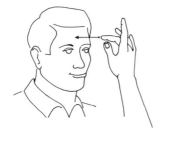

FEEL 388

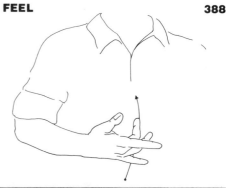

SYMPATHY (DM), PITY (DM) 389

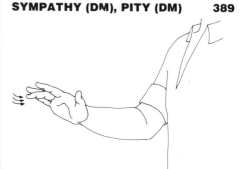

HEART 390

TASTE, (DELICIOUS) 391

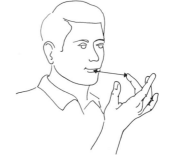

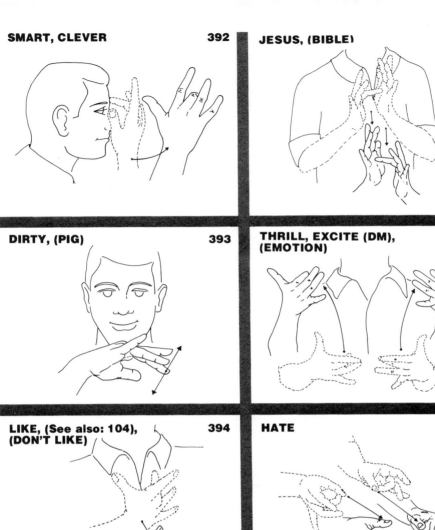

SMART, CLEVER   392

JESUS, (BIBLE)   396

DIRTY, (PIG)   393

THRILL, EXCITE (DM), (EMOTION)   397

LIKE, (See also: 104), (DON'T LIKE)   394

HATE   398

INTERESTING   395

DICTIONARY (DM)   399

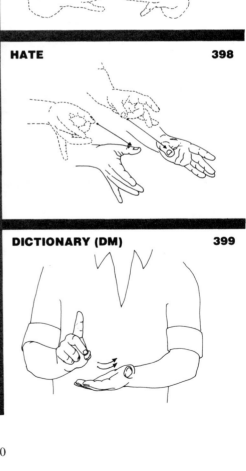

LESSON 29

ODD, STRANGE, PECULIAR 400

HUNT (DM), SEARCH (DM), LOOK FOR (DM) 401

SCREAM, SHOUT 402

DRINK 403

WISH, (HUNGRY) 404

MARRY, (MARRIAGE) 405

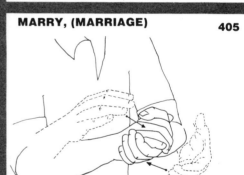

ENGAGEMENT 406

61

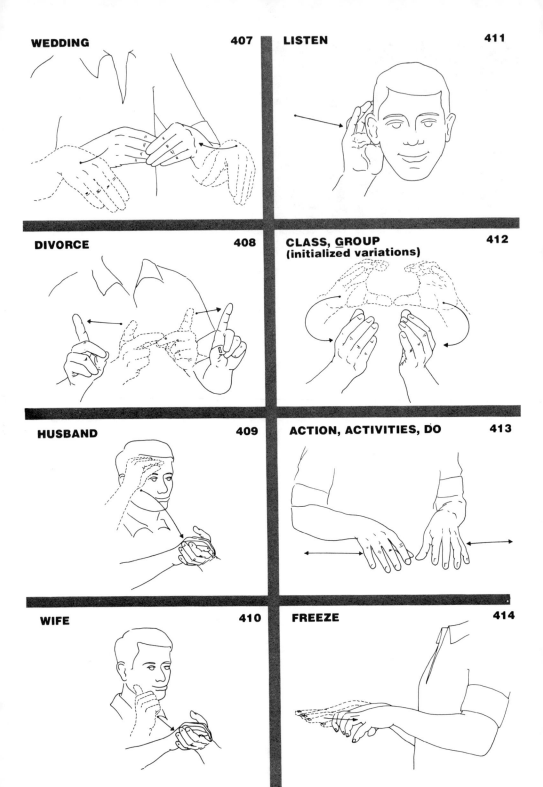

WEDDING 407

LISTEN 411

DIVORCE 408

CLASS, GROUP 412
(initialized variations)

HUSBAND 409

ACTION, ACTIVITIES, DO 413

WIFE 410

FREEZE 414

LESSON 30

IDEA, (IMAGINE) 418

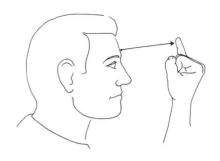

ITALY, ITALIAN 415

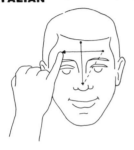

JEALOUS, ENVIOUS 419

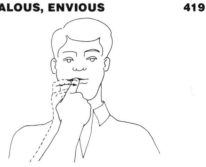

CATHOLIC 416

DREAM 420

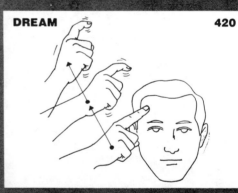

INSTITUTION, RESIDENTIAL 417
(Deaf schools)

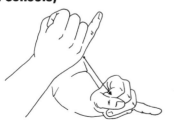

JAPAN, JAPANESE 421

CHINA, CHINESE 422

LOAF, (VACATION), (RETIRE) 425

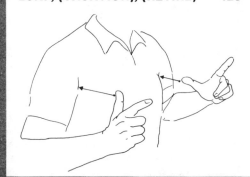

LAST (See also: 205), (FINAL) 423

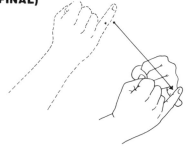

PERSON, (INDIVIDUAL) 426

PEOPLE 427

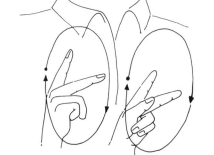

LESSON 31

LAZY 424

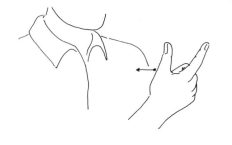

DOCTOR, PSYCHIATRIST, NURSE 428

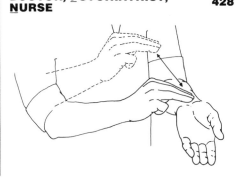

LARGE, BIG 429

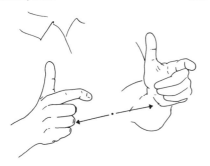

PLACE (See also: 252), POSITION, AREA 433

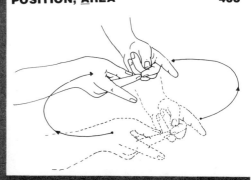

SMALL, LITTLE 430

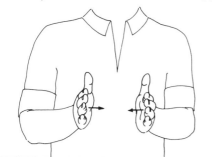

LESSON 32

PERFECT, (EXACT, PRECISELY) 431

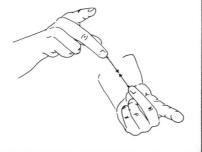

GREEN 434

PERMISSION, PRIVILEGE 432

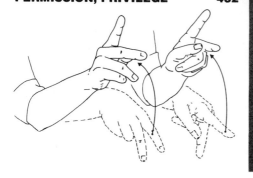

BROWN 435

RED   436

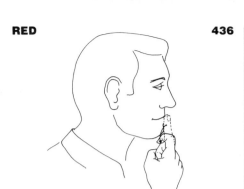

ORANGE   440

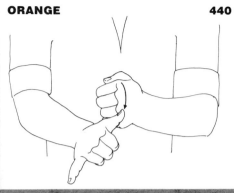

BLUE   437

PINK   441

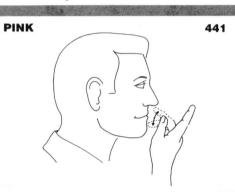

YELLOW   438

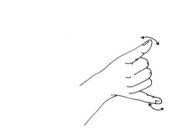

GRAY   442

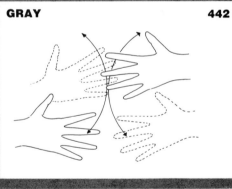

PURPLE   439

WASHINGTON (D.C. and George) 443

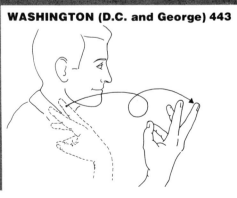

66

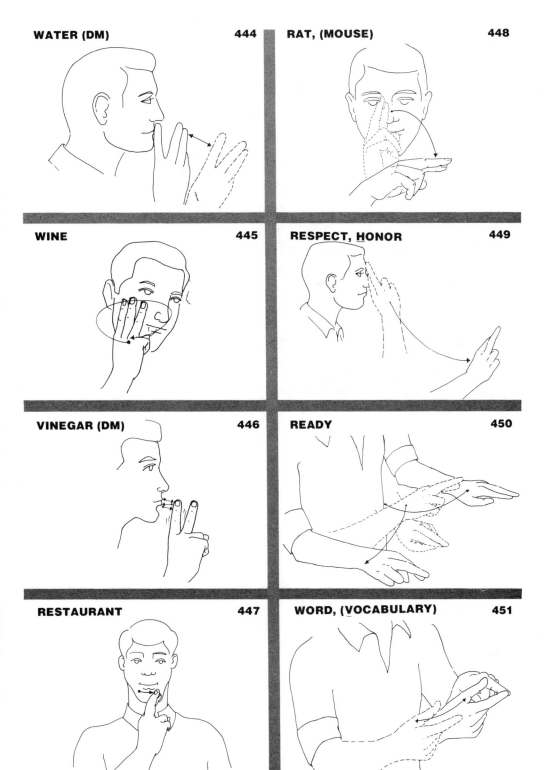

WATER (DM) 444

RAT, (MOUSE) 448

WINE 445

RESPECT, HONOR 449

VINEGAR (DM) 446

READY 450

RESTAURANT 447

WORD, (VOCABULARY) 451

WORLD 452

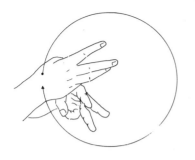

PRAISE, CONGRATULATIONS 455

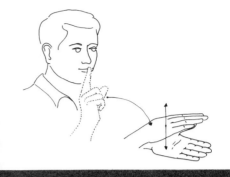

LESSON 33

PROMISE 456

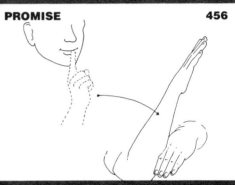

DEAF 453

DISAPPEAR, (APPEAR) 457
(See also: 203), (ESCAPE)

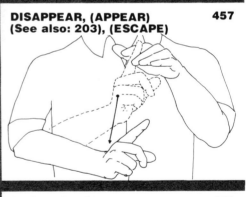

HOPE, EXPECT 454

BEGIN, START 458

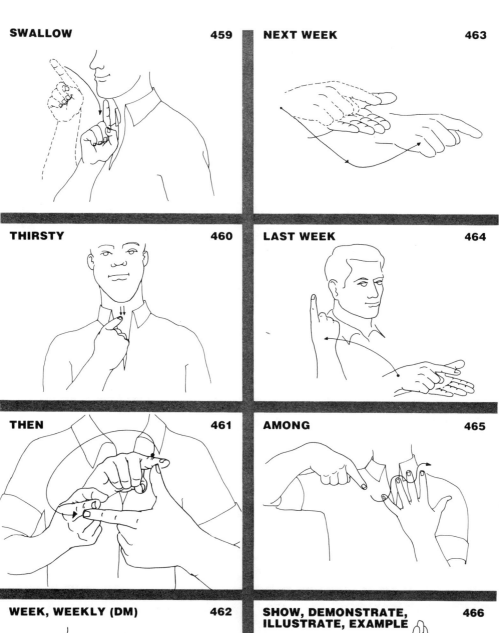

SWALLOW   459

NEXT WEEK   463

THIRSTY   460

LAST WEEK   464

THEN   461

AMONG   465

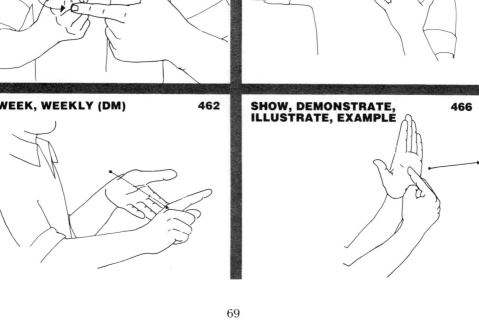

WEEK, WEEKLY (DM)   462

SHOW, DEMONSTRATE, ILLUSTRATE, EXAMPLE   466

PAY 467

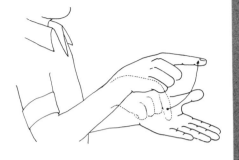

DISCUSS, DEBATE, ARGUE 471
(See also: 325)

ONCE, (SOMETIMES (DM), 468
OCCASIONALLY (DM))

CANCEL, (CRITICIZE), 472
(CORRECT
(See also: 226))

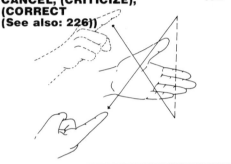

DEBT, OWE 469

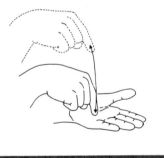

TALL 473

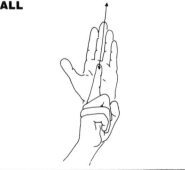

MAJOR, (OCCUPATION), 470
SPECIALTY, PROFESSION, FIELD

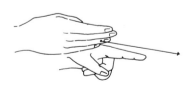

NORTH, (SOUTH, etc.) 474

BELIEVE, (FAITH) 475

CONDENSE, ABBREVIATE, SUMMARIZE 478

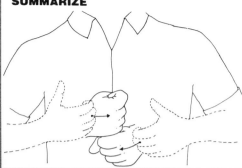

LESSON 34

MILK (DM) 479

GUESS, (MISS) (See also: 223) 476

ENGLAND, ENGLISH 480

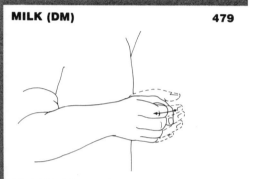

PRESIDENT, SUPERINTENDENT 477

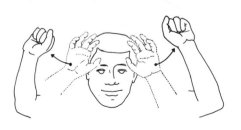

CHURCH, TEMPLE 481

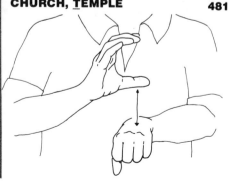

71

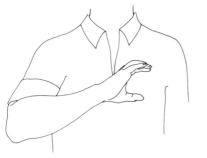

GLASS, (CUP) 483

GROW, SPRING (DM) 487

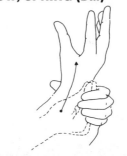

RELIGION 484

LESSON 35

OLD, AGE 485

PICTURE 488

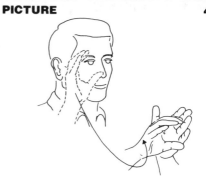

FAT 489

USE UP, DEPLETE 490

EARN, COLLECT, INCOME 491

REMOVE, (SUBTRACT) 492

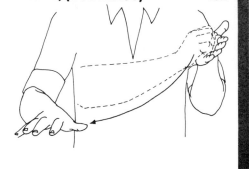

CREAM 493

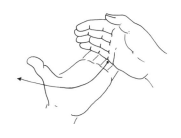

MAGAZINE, BOOKLET, PAMPHLET 494

COUNT, ADD UP 495

MEAT 496

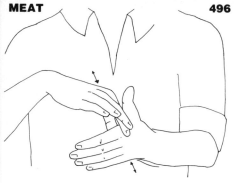

GRAVY, GREASE (DM) 497

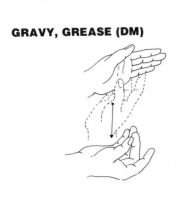

FIND, DISCOVER, PICK UP 501

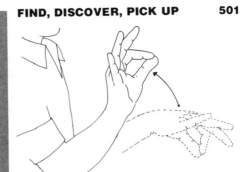

DUTY (DM) 498

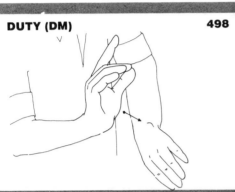

PICK OUT, SELECT, CHOOSE 502

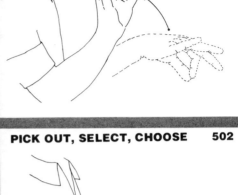

HONEST 499

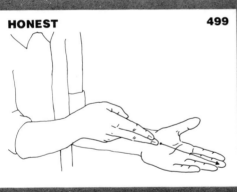

PRINT (DM) 503

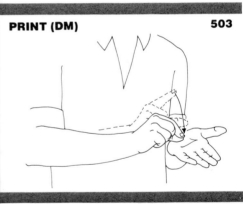

REGISTER, SIGN, 500
(See also: 112) SIGNATURE

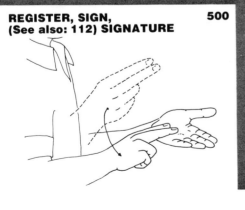

GRADUATE, CERTIFICATE 504

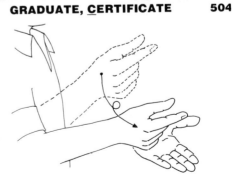

LESSON 36

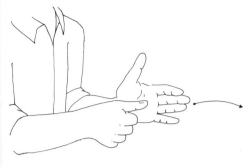

EMPHASIZE **508**

BETTER **505**

ESTABLISH, SET UP **509**

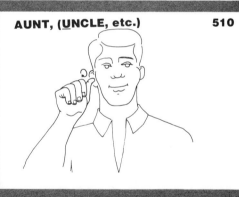

BEST

AUNT, (UNCLE, etc.) **510**

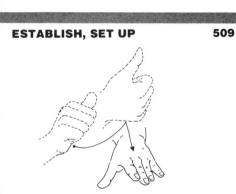

IMPRESS **507**

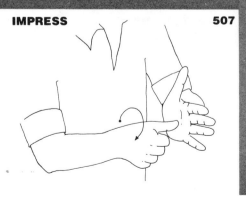

LETTER, MAIL **511**

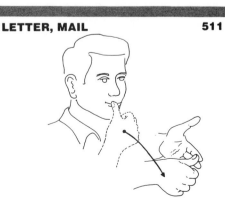

STAMP (noun) 512

PRACTICE, TRAIN (verb) 513
(See also: 311)

LEAD, GUIDE 514

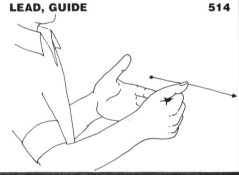

FIRST 515

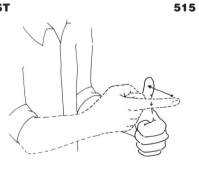

ABILITY, SKILL, EXPERTNESS 516

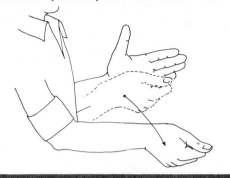

FORGET, FORGETFUL (DM) 517

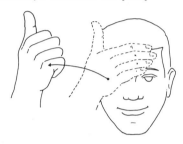

LESSON 37

BUSINESS, (BUSY) 518

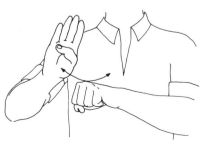

STUDY 519

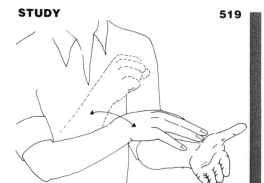

RULE 520

CONSTITUTION 521

LAW 522

FORBID 523

PRINCIPLE 524

AGAINST, OPPOSE 525

HELP, AID, ASSIST 526

77

SUPPORT, (FOUNDATION) 527

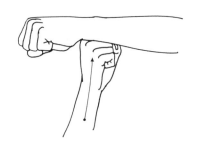

LATER, AFTER A WHILE 531

ASSISTANT (DM) 528

MINUTE 532

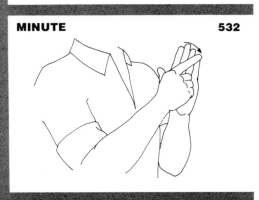

SING, MUSIC, POETRY, SONG 529

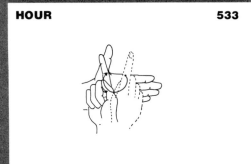

HOUR 533

DANCE, PARTY (See also: 650) 530

PLENTY, (ENOUGH (DM)) 534

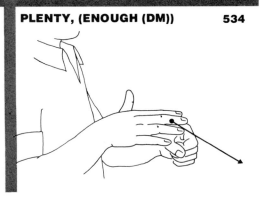

FILL, FULLY, COMPLETELY 535

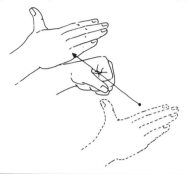

LESSON 38

DRAW, ART, <u>D</u>ESIGN 536

PAINT 537

FULL 538

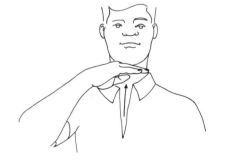

FRANCE, FRENCH 539

CAT (DM) 540

SPIRIT, SOUL, GHOST 541

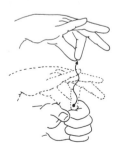

IMPORTANT, (WORTH, VALUE) 542

MANAGE, CONTROL, DIRECT 546

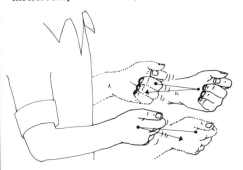

JOIN, (See also: 615) BELONG 543

TEA 547

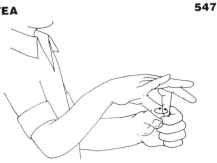

COOPERATE, (RELATE) 544

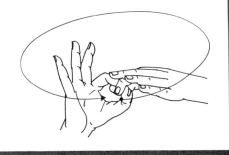

AWFUL, TERRIBLE 548

EXPLAIN, DESCRIBE 545

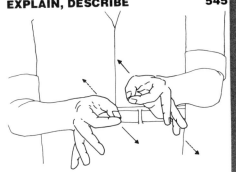

INSTEAD OF 549

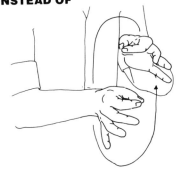

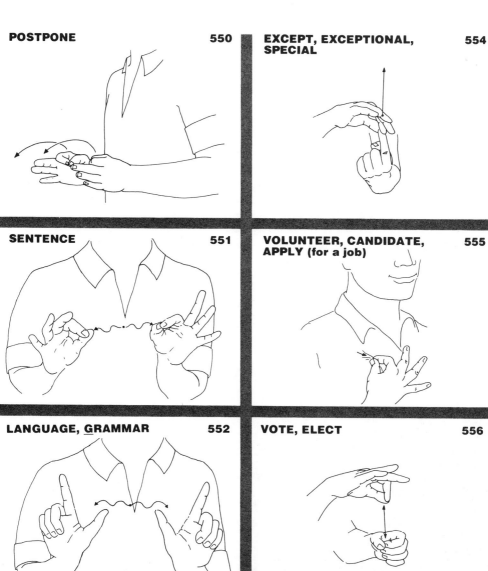

POSTPONE 550

EXCEPT, EXCEPTIONAL, SPECIAL 554

SENTENCE 551

VOLUNTEER, CANDIDATE, APPLY (for a job) 555

LANGUAGE, GRAMMAR 552

VOTE, ELECT 556

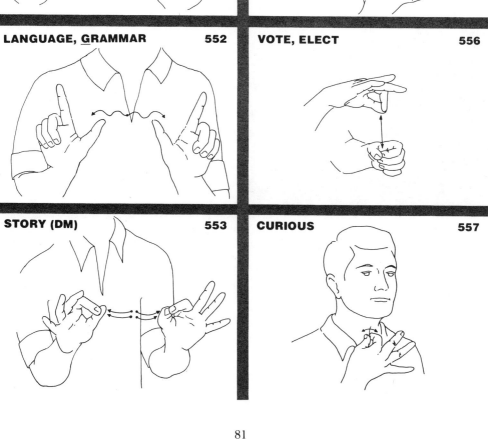

STORY (DM) 553

CURIOUS 557

DECIDE, DETERMINE 558

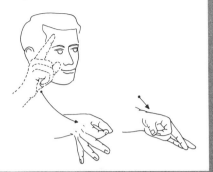

COURT, (JUDGMENT), (JUDGE) 559

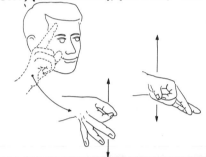

LESSON 39

PUNISHMENT, PENALTY 560

TAX, COST, CHARGE 561

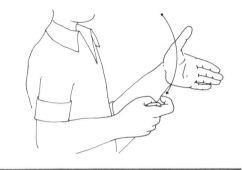

DEMAND, TAKES, REQUIRES 562

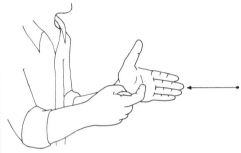

KEY (DM) 563

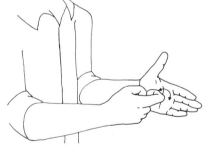

LOCK 564

MEAN (See also: 334) 565

KNEEL 569

PURPOSE, INTENT 566

FALL 570

BRIDGE 567

LIE (lie down) 571

STAND, (ARISE) 568

FAIL 572

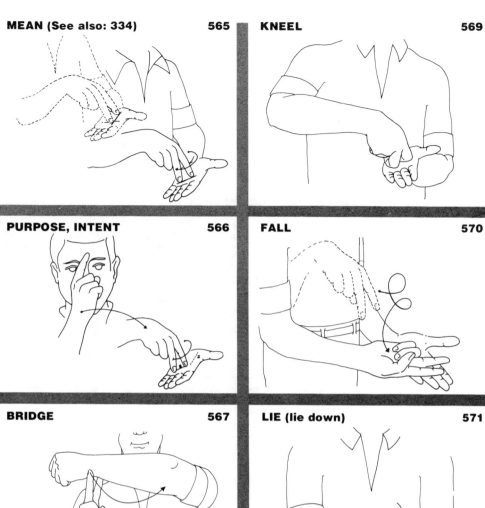
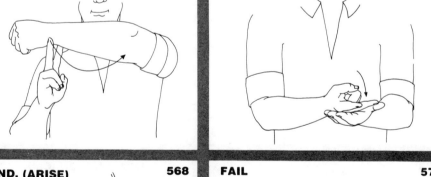
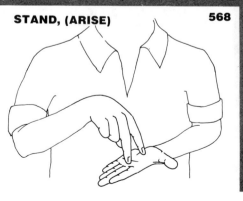
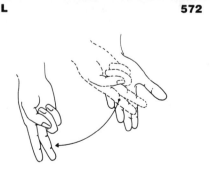

SLIP 573

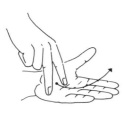

RUN 577

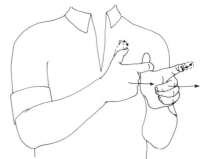

HOP 574

LESSON 40

JUMP 575

WEAK 578

WALK 576

LEARN, EDUCATION (DM), 579
(learn + person = student)

COPY, IMITATE 580

PENCIL 584

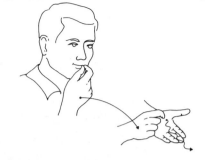

TELEGRAM, WIRE 581

READ 585

MEDICINE 582

SECRETARY 586

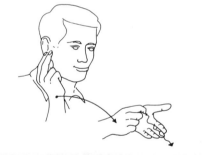

WRITE 583

MOVIE 587

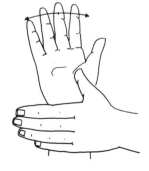

85

LESSON 41

POISON 591

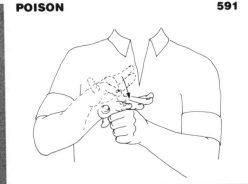

DUMB 588

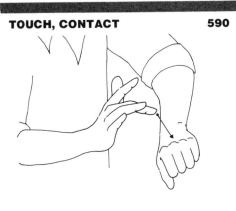

WIN 592

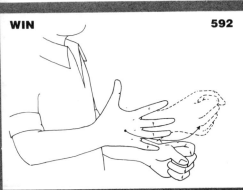

GIVE UP, SURRENDER 589

CELEBRATE, (VICTORY) 593

TOUCH, CONTACT 590

GERMAN, GERMANY 594

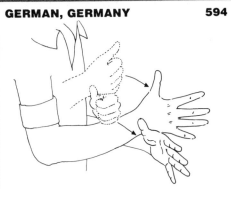

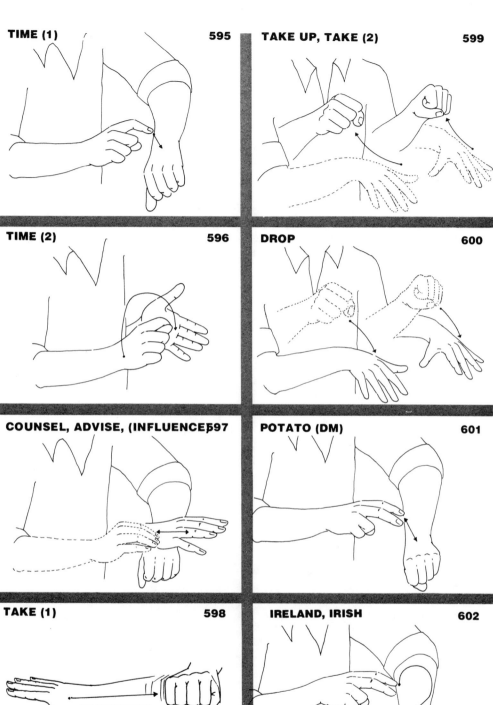

TIME (1)   595

TIME (2)   596

COUNSEL, ADVISE, (INFLUENCE) 597

TAKE (1)   598

TAKE UP, TAKE (2)   599

DROP   600

POTATO (DM)   601

IRELAND, IRISH   602

TRAVEL 603

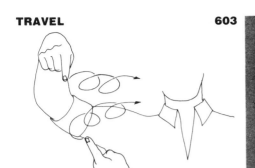

VACANT, EMPTY, BARE, NUDE, BLANK, (BALD) 607

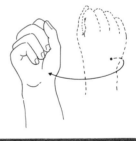

GET (See also: 280), RECEIVE 604

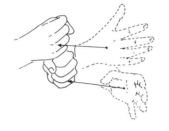

YES (DM) 608

CATCH 605

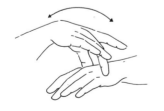

STRIKE, REBELLION, REVOLT 609

EARTH, GEOGRAPHY 606

LESSON 42

SHORT 613

FUNNY (DM) 610

HOSPITAL, INFIRMARY, PATIENT 614

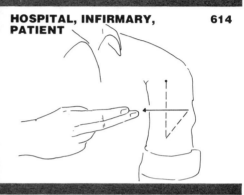

FUN 611

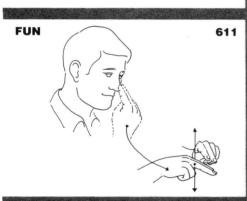

QUIT, (PARTICIPATE, JOIN) 615
(See also: 543)

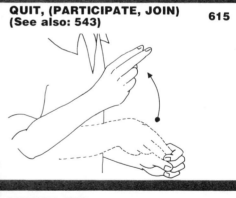

HURRY 612

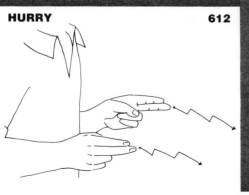

BUTTER (DM) 616

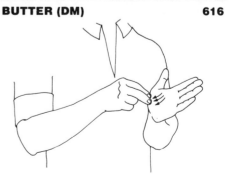

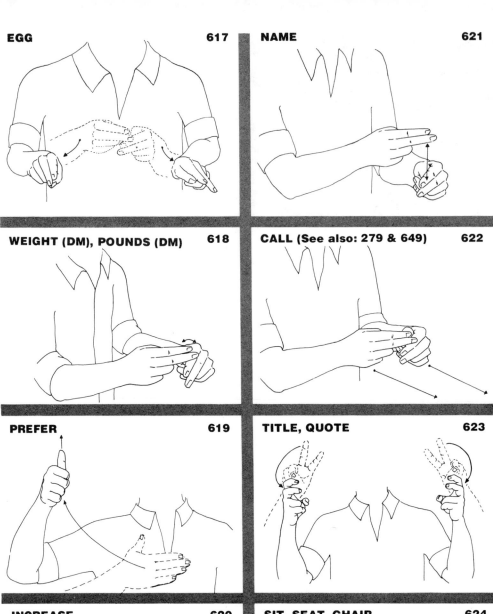

EGG   617

NAME   621

WEIGHT (DM), POUNDS (DM)   618

CALL (See also: 279 & 649)   622

PREFER   619

TITLE, QUOTE   623

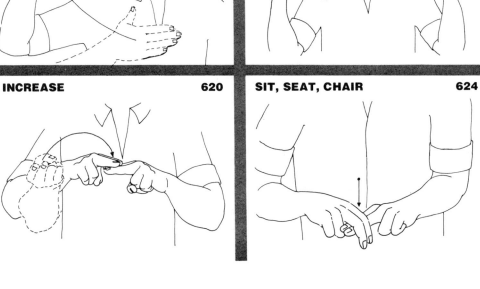

INCREASE   620

SIT, SEAT, CHAIR   624

HISTORY 625

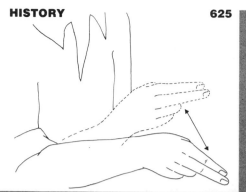

MUST, (NEED, OUGHT, SHOULD), 628
HAVE TO

USE, WEAR 626

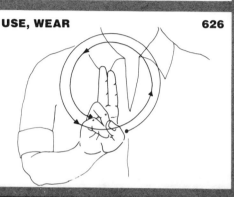

DAMAGE, RUIN, (TEASE (DM)) 629

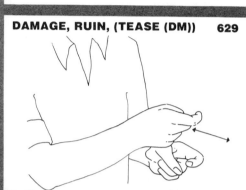

LESSON 43

TEST 630

SPAIN, SPANISH 627

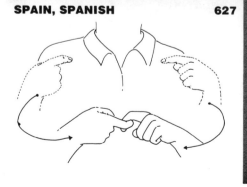

ASK (See also: 188), QUESTION 631

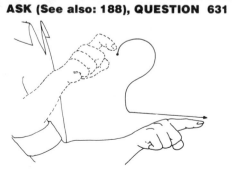

DRY, DULL, BORING 632

SUSPECT (DM) 636

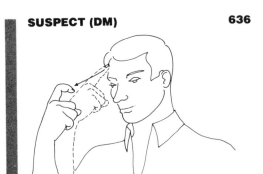

UGLY 633

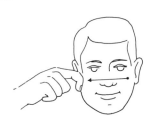

NOTICE 637

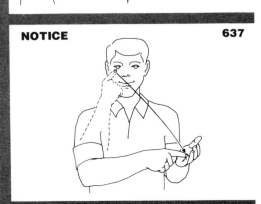

SUMMER 634

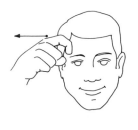

FRIEND 638

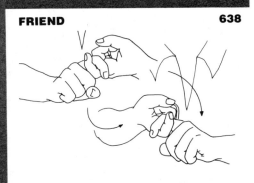

WISE, (MIND) 635

RELATIVE 639

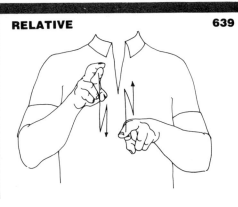

PHYSICS 640

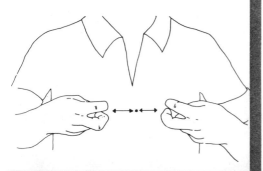

ELECTRICITY 641

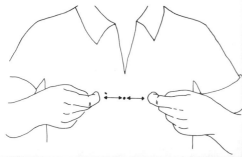

LESSON 44

COUNTRY 642

SHAVE 643

WRONG, MISTAKE, ERROR 644

STILL 645

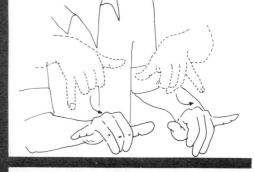

MEASURE 646

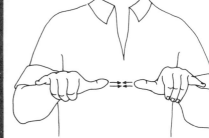

CONTINUE, LASTING, (STAY) 647

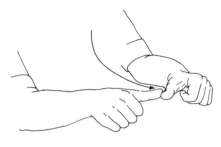

LESSON 45

SILLY (DM), FOOL, RIDICULOUS 648

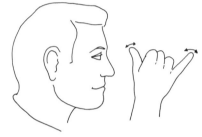

AIRPLANE, FLY 651

TELEPHONE, CALL 649
(See also: 279 & 622)

GREECE, GREEK 652

PLAY (See also: 123), 650
PARTY (See also: 530)

GALLAUDET, GLASSES (DM) 653

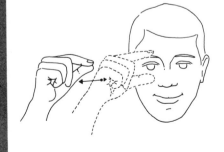

TICKET 654

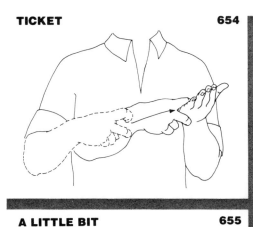

HOW MUCH, HOW MANY 658

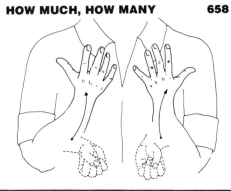

A LITTLE BIT 655

HIDE 659

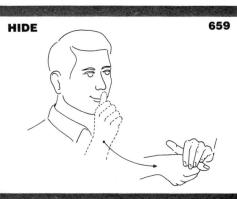

FAST, QUICK 656

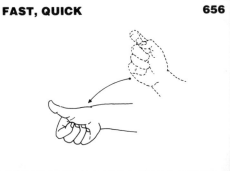

GOSSIP 660

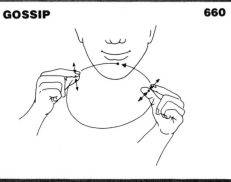

MANY (DM) 657

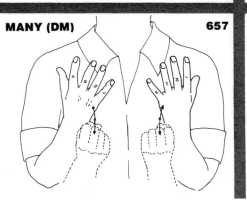

BOTH 661

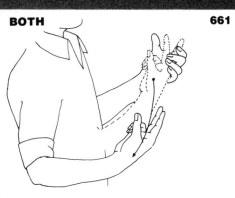

REVENGE   662

CHANGE, (REVERSE)   663

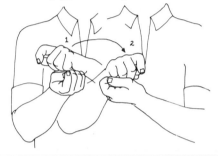

SURPRISE, (AWAKE, WAKE UP) 664

PRONOUNS

SHE 668

HE 665

HER 669

HIM 666

HERS 670

HIS 667

IT 671

97

THEIR 672

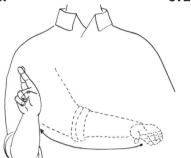

WE (See also: 4) 676

THEM 673

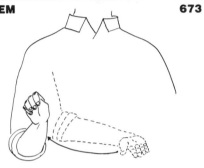

AFFIXES

THEY 674

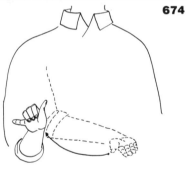

-ABLE 677

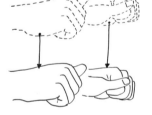

OUR (See also: 7) 675

-AGE 678

-DOM 679

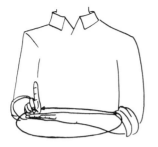

ENT 683

DUR- 680

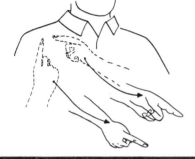

-ER, -OR, -AR 684

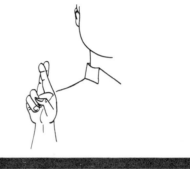

-ED & past tense 681

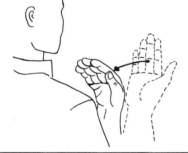

-ESS 685

-EN & past participle 682

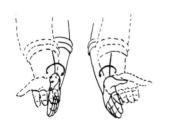

-EST (See also: 128) 686

-IC 687

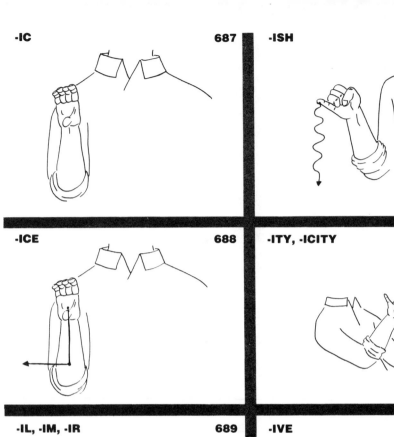

-ISH 691

-ICE 688

-ITY, -ICITY 692

-IL, -IM, -IR 689

-IVE 693

-ING 690

-LY 694

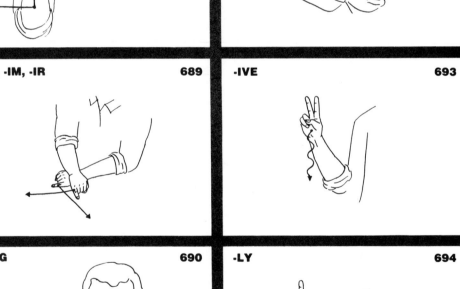

100

-MENT 695

-STEAD- 699

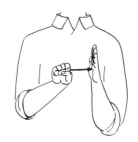

-NESS 696

-TION, -ION 700

-OUS 697

-URE 701

-S 698

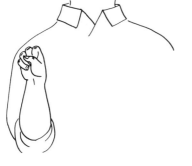

-Y 702

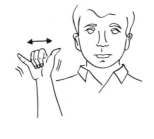

·YOND· 703

CONTRACTIONS

'D 704

'LL 705

'M 706

N'T 707

'RE 708

'S 709

'VE 710

ARTICLES

A 711

AN 712

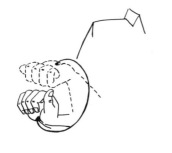

THE 713

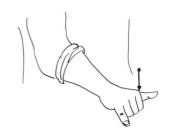

THIS (See also: 23) 714

THAT (See also: 22) 715

THESE 716

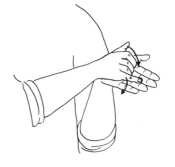

103

THOSE (See also: 24) 717

BE 720

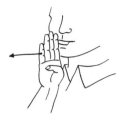

IS 721

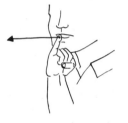

THE VERB "TO BE"

AM 718

WAS 722

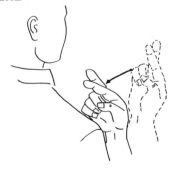

ARE 719

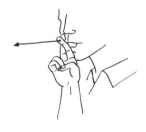

WERE 723

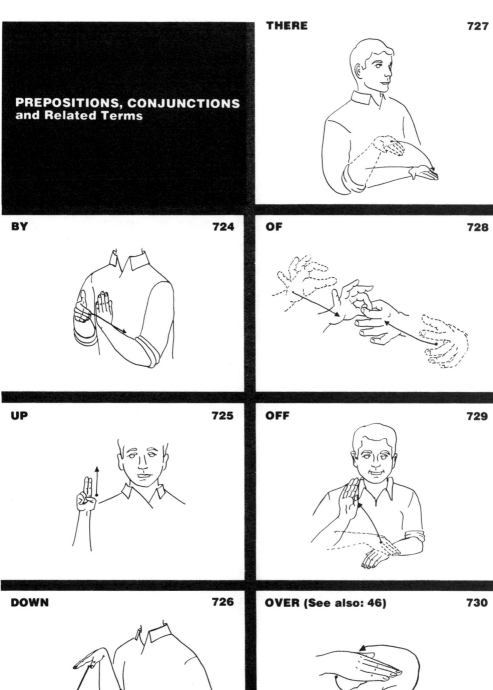

**PREPOSITIONS, CONJUNCTIONS
and Related Terms**

THERE 727

BY 724

OF 728

UP 725

OFF 729

DOWN 726

OVER (See also: 46) 730

105

TOO 731

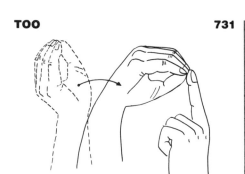

RATHER 735

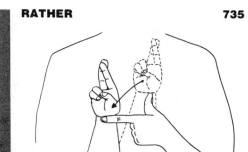

EVER 732

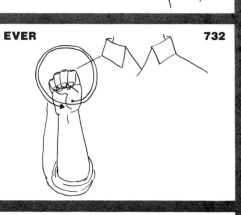

WHETHER (See also: 130) 736

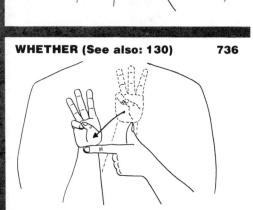

EITHER 733

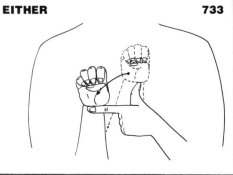

ELSE (See also: 91) 737

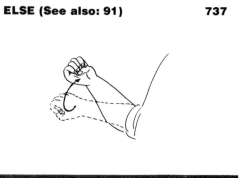

OR 734

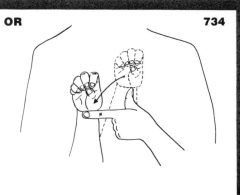

LESSON 1

Practice material for Lesson 1 will be found in *LaVera M. Guillory's* book, *"Expressive and Receptive Fingerspelling for Hearing Adults,"* published by *Claitor's Publishing Division, Baton Rouge, Louisiana* and available for $1.50 from *the National Association of the Deaf and the Publisher*. The practice material is designed to facilitate both sending and receiving of the manual alphabet. All students are advised to secure copies of Mrs. G's book as an adjunct to this text which is concerned mostly with basic signs.

LESSON 2

1. Count one, two, three, four, five.
2. I have ten fingers.
3. Can you multiply 2 by 4?
4. What is 40 plus 8?
5. They came 1 by 1.
6. Sing, "Tea for Two."
7. Avoid the number 13.
8. Count to fifteen.
9. Lend me 20 cents.
10. I am 98 years old.
11. It's not worth 2 cents.
12. She's sweet 16.
13. Two bits is 25 cents.
14. "The end" is written "30".
15. They were married 50 years.
16. Lesson three is easy.
17. We ate at 12.
18. Bedtime is 9 p.m.
19. Stay on Route 66.
20. What's 70 plus 17?
21. That's 87.
22. "99 out of 100 wanna be kissed."
23. Let's play 500.
24. A "G" note is 1000 dollars.
25. 50,000,000 Frenchmen could be wrong!
26. Did Nixon win in 1972?
27. Call the cops at 444-1111.
28. The house number was fifty-two-oh-eight.
29. These dates are historically important: 1492, 1776, 1812, 1865, 1898, 1918, 1941, and 1945.
30. I have three-hundred-seventy-five dollars.
31. One-hundred-sixty-seven horseshoes were thrown.
32. 5 times 8 is 40.
33. We saw twenty-eight-million-two-hundred-thousand-three-hundred-twelve boys.
34. Fifty-four is our magic number.
35. I was 21 yesterday.
36. He spent twenty minutes waiting.
37. My mother is still 35.

LESSON 3

1. *I* want to learn signs.
2. Please come to see *me*.
3. *I* have a letter for *you*. (Singular)
4. *I* want to see all of *you*. (Plural)
5. *We* hope to finish this book soon.
6. Come with *us*.
7. *My* cat is white.
8. This book is *mine*.
9. Come to *our* house.
10. The blue car is *ours*.
11. *Your* book has come. (Singular)
12. *Your* books have come. (Plural)
13. *I* like to go by *myself*.
14. *You* may go by *yourselves*.
15. *You* should do this *yourself*.
16. *We* will go by *ourselves*.
17. *Who* was that?
18. *Whom* do *you* know?
19. *Whose* pad is this?

LESSON 4

1. *He could not* go *because he* was sick.
2. *Since he* was sick, *he could not* go.
3. *I* left *my* keys *in* the car.
4. *What* is *inside* the box?
5. Let the cat *out*.
6. *I* am going *outside*.
7. *Why* didn't *you* call?
8. Leave *your* book *on my* desk.
9. *I* will get it *for* you.
10. *We* can do *our* shopping *together*.
11. *Accompany him* to the jail.
12. Put it *with* the boxes.
13. *I* can do *this without you*.
14. *Where* did *you* get *that* tan?
15. Can *you* do *this* now?
16. *Those* books belong to *me*.
17. *What* is *your* name?
18. *But how* will *I* get there?
19. Her recipe is *different from mine*.
20. *Where* do they live?
21. *How* are *you*?
22. *I* want *to* wait *until* he comes home.
23. *I* will drive *to* New York.
24. *We* were going *toward* the airport.
25. *When* are *you* leaving?

26. These roses are *from my* garden.
27. The dog is *under* the bed.
28. *We* slept *beneath* the tree.
29. It is *in the basement.*
30. *We* flew *above* the clouds.
31. It is *below* freezing.
32. He will *enter* next.
33. *You* may come *into* the room now.

LESSON 5

1. I *won't* see her tonight.
2. He *wouldn't* take any.
3. He *refuses* to do that.
4. I *can't* be there at *that* time.
5. *Why couldn't you* go?
6. *That's impossible!*
7. *We* have *nothing* to do.
8. *None* of the apples was good.
9. There is *no* mail *for me* today.
10. *My* answer to *that* is *no.*
11. I *was told not* to do *that.*
12. *Don't* do that.
13. He *doesn't* want to do it.
14. She *isn't* going to school today.
15. I *deny* cheating.
16. I *never* saw him again.

LESSON 6

1. *We* walked *across* the street.
2. The bridge goes *over* the road.
3. *You* may leave *now.*
4. *Clean your* desk, please.
5. *We* met some *nice* people *on* the trip.
6. I hate *cleaning* the stove.
7. *Clean up your* mess.
8. *Where* is *your* school?
9. *What* is the name of *your college?*
10. I go *to* Southern *University.*
11. After the game, *perhaps we* can go.
12. *Maybe our* team will win.
13. I *might* try to stop by today.
14. I *probably* will buy a house soon.
15. Will *you bring* some coffee, please?
16. I *brought* some flowers *for you.*
17. I *carried my* cat *to* the car.
18. *What* do *you* have to *offer?*
19. Ken *proposed* to move the fence.
20. *Stop* doing *that!*
21. The car *stopped* in time.
22. She is a good *cook.*
23. I *almost* sprained *my* ankle.
24. *It* is *easy* to say *that.*
25. Are *you comfortable* in *that* chair?
26. I will be *here until* tomorrow.

27. I need some *paper.*
28. *All right, we* will go *to* the movies.
29. *You* have a *right* to do *that.*
30. *Some* of the members *could not* come.
31. He read *part* of the book.
32. *You* will need more *money* than *that.*
33. He is a very *wealthy* man.
34. *That* coat cost *me 50 dollars.*
35. Let *us buy* some food.
36. *We* bought a *new* car recently.
37. He *spent his money* on horses.
38. *That* was a *cheap* dress she was wearing.
39. Her clothes are *expensive.*
40. *Don't waste your* food.
41. The rabbit ran *through* the woods.
42. Let us go through the *lesson* once more.
43. We are on *chapter* 6 *now.*
44. Taking a *course* is much work.
45. *Pardon me.*
46. *What* is *your excuse this* time?
47. I *forgive you.*
48. Class is *dismissed.*
49. He *doesn't* work *because* he was *laid off.*
50. *We* bought a *new* house.
51. *What* does the *paragraph* say?
52. I made up *my* grocery *list.*
53. *List* some of the things *we* need.
54. John caught *seven fish* yesterday.

LESSON 7

1. *I think I* will stay home.
2. *What* are *you thinking* about?
3. He was *wondering what* to do.
4. I have a *reason for that.*
5. *How long have you* been deaf?
6. Can *you hear* the bell?
7. I am *always* late.
8. He was the *only* man there.
9. His *face* was ashen.
10. *We* liked her *looks.*
11. Can *you understand* French?
12. Albert Einstein was an *intelligent* man.
13. *My* brother is *brilliant.*
14. Her dress was *black.*

LESSON 8

1. *Memorize* the *lesson.*
2. I see him *everyday (daily).*
3. *Do you* have *another* dime?
4. It rained the *other* day.
5. *What else* can *I* do?
6. I will see *you tomorrow.*
7. It was hot *yesterday.*
8. I am *sorry* about *that.*

9. She has much *pride.*
10. *We* are *proud* of *you.*
11. He had a serious *operation.*
12. Do *you* have *any money?*
13. *Where* is *my handkerchief?*
14. She has a bad *cold.*
15. *I* drove *to Canada* last year.
16. Can *you* keep a *secret?*
17. Have *patience with me.*
18. *How* can *you bear* the pain?
19. *How* can *you endure this* heat?
20. He *suffered* much pain.

LESSON 9

1. *During* the night it rained.
2. *While I* work, *you* can study.
3. *Since you* are early, *we* can *probably* start now.
4. *I* have *not* seen him *lately.*
5. They are *alike in* their tastes.
6. *Your* car is *like my* car.
7. *He* said the *same* thing.
8. John *also* came.
9. The tall *boy* is *my* son.
10. *Male* fish are pretty.
11. She is a pretty *girl.*
12. *Female* flies reproduce.
13. *I* have only *one brother.*
14. *My sister* is younger than *my brother.*
15. *That* man is very *famous.*
16. *About* how much did *it* cost?
17. He *comes around* very often.
18. She *signs* very well.
19. *Come as you* are.
20. Please *go to* the store *for me.*
21. Please *answer my* letter.

LESSON 10

1. *Wash my* dirty socks, please.
2. Have *you washed your* clothes?
3. *I washed* the dishes last night.
4. *Most* people *bathe* once a day.
5. *My bath* is usually a shower.
6. Do *you remember* Ruth?
7. *No, my memory* is failing.
8. *Where* do *you live?*
9. *Whose residence* is *this?*
10. *What* is your *address?*
11. *Life* is very funny.
12. They have been *sweethearts since* high school.
13. Do *you associate with* deaf people?
14. *We mingled with* the crowd.
15. *We like each other* very much.

16. Do *you like drama?*
17. *We* went *to* the *play* last night.
18. The *acting* was very good.
19. He has much *ambition.*
20. *She* is an *ambitious* young lady.
21. Do *you* play *cards?*
22. He *deals* very fast.
23. *You* must *follow me.*
24. The cops *chased* the robber.
25. He *avoided* the police.
26. *I* am trying to *catch up.*
27. *We passed your* house *yesterday.*
28. *Most* people live *in* the city.
29. *That* is the *newest* house *on* the block.
30. *My coat* is old.
31. *I* do *not* know *whether to go* or *not.*
32. *Which* man is *your* father?
33. *You* may *have whichever you* want.
34. *Substitute* tea *for* coffee.
35. *We exchanged* prisoners.
36. *We traded* books.
37. *Each* of *us* was late.
38. *Every boy* should have the book.
39. *My son likes science.*

LESSON 11

1. He is very *polite.*
2. I feel *fine.*
3. The tea is *hot!*
4. It is *warm in this* room.
5. *My mother* is *not* well.
6. *My grandmother* is very old.
7. *My father came from* Russia.
8. Her *parents* are away *on* a trip.
9. *My grandfather looked* like Santa Claus.
10. *Where* did *that woman* go?
11. *Who* was *that lady I* saw *you with?*
12. *Most men like* to play poker.
13. The *gentleman* was nice *to us.*
14. The *children* are happy *school* is over.
15. Can *you fingerspell that* word?
16. *How* do *you spell your* name?
17. *What* is the *color* of her *new* rug?
18. *I complained* to the police.
19. Do *you* have a *gripe?*
20. The teacher was *cross with us.*
21. *I* was *irritated with* the traffic.

LESSON 12

1. *Those* new *shoes* are ugly.
2. It is *my custom* to drink coffee at *10 o'clock.*
3. *I try* to break bad *habits.*
4. He made *no attempt* to call *me.*
5. *We* must *try to go* early.

6. The team made a great *effort*.
7. *You may* see *him now.*
8. *Can you come tomorrow?*
9. He *is able* to do many things.
10. *That* is quite *possible*.
11. Did *you break* the window?
12. *I doubt that we can* both go.
13. *I don't like cold* weather.
14. *We* had a mild *winter*.
15. *Exercise* is good *for you*.
16. *My car* is a Ford.
17. *Don't drive* so fast.
18. Some people *work very hard*.

LESSON 13

1. *You look* very *sad!*
2. *Where* is the *fire?*
3. *I burned* the roast.
4. Do *you like basketball?*
5. The patient is *nervous about* his *operation.*
6. *In what* part of *America* do *you* live?
7. *Much of what you* say is true.
8. *Remember* to take a *shower.*
9. Will *you wait for me?*
10. The party was very *noisy.*
11. Wear *your* blue *pants.*
12. *This* store carries *expensive dresses.*
13. *You* have so many *clothes.*
14. *I want* a trip *to* Europe.
15. *We don't want any* trouble.
16. *I finished my work.*
17. I have *already seen* the movie.
18. *Leave your* coat *on* the bed.
19. The *football* season will soon be here.
20. *Do not frighten* the birds.
21. The storm *scared me.*
22. Are *you afraid* of the dark?
23. *I have a fear* of dogs.

LESSON 14

1. *Open* the package, please.
2. *Close your book now.*
3. *My book* is *about signs.*
4. It is a good *day* to *go to* the beach.
5. Good *morning!*
6. Shall *we go* at *noon?*
7. Babies nap *in the afternoon.*
8. It gets cool at *night.*
9. *I* was up *all night with* a toothache.
10. He *styed overnight* at the motel.
11. Did *you ask* her to *come?*
12. The family *requests no* flowers.
13. *We all prayed for* the safe return of *our* P.O.W.'s.

14. He seems very *enthusiastic.*
15. The *table* is walnut.
16. *Your desk* is messy.
17. He wrote the story *again* and *again.*
18. Would *you repeat that,* please?
19. *We often go to* the beach.
20. *All* of *us* should go.
21. The *whole* staff agrees.
22. Should *we include* the Smiths?
23. He *became* more *involved* in *his* work.
24. *I* need *more* sugar *for my* coffee.
25. *We should go, anyway (regardless).*
26. It *does not matter to me.*
27. *No matter what* the weather is, *we* should go.
28. *When* will *you leave for* Europe?
29. He *departed* too soon.
30. *Compare my* work *with yours.*
31. Did *you lose your* ring?

LESSON 15

1. His *lecture* was *on science.*
2. *Many* people heard his *speech.*
3. He *preaches every* Sunday.
4. The *future seems* bleak.
5. *Will you* go?
6. *Shall we* leave *now?*
7. *What* is *that thing?*
8. It *seems* dark *in* there.
9. It *appears* to be a good book.
10. *Apparently,* she *could not come.*
11. It *looks like* rain.
12. I went *before you came.*
13. Do *you* live *in* the *past* or the present?
14. *Last* night *we* went *to* a movie.
15. Many years *ago we* had few cars.
16. He was *formerly in* prison.
17. *Previously, I worked in* New York City.
18. *I know your father* and *mother.*
19. *I don't know* the *answer.*

LESSON 16

1. *May I see you* a moment?
2. *My* friend is *blind* in *one* eye.
3. *Look at* the swans *in* the lake.
4. *Watch yourself in* the mirror.
5. *He is careless with his money.*
6. *His voice* is so loud.
7. *Some* people *lipread* very well.
8. Do *you go to* an *oral school?*
9. *He* is an *ignorant* person.
10. *Some* people are very *stupid.*

11. *Do not misunderstand me.*
12. The thief *stole my* purse.

LESSON 17

1. *Some* of *us don't have* good *speech.*
2. Did she *say what* she wanted?
3. He *said* he would *come.*
4. *I spoke to* him *about* the *course.*
5. *I talked with* her *about our* plans.
6. He *wants* to *tell you* a story.
7. The radio *announced* the smog alert.
8. It is *true that I* am deaf.
9. *Which* is the *real thing?*
10. *I* am *sure* he is *right.*
11. It was a *lonely night.*
12. *I* was *alone last night.*
13. Pickles are *sour.*
14. He is a *bitter man now.*
15. *I* will *try not* to *disappoint you.*
16. I *miss my* family.
17. It was a *false* alarm.
18. *Some* people *smile all* the *time.*
19. He *laughed* at the joke.
20. *This* sentence is *correct.*
21. *Which one is right?*
22. *We* visit *each other regularly.*
23. The little girl *cried* and *cried.*
24. Did *you see* the *tears on* the doll?
25. *When* did *this happen?*
26. Such *things* do *occur in* real *life.*
27. Would *you come* and *meet* him?
28. To *succeed one must* work hard.
29. *I agree with you.*
30. *I want* to *have* a *talk with you.*
31. *They* had a *long conversatior*

LESSON 18

1. The trees are *pretty in* the fall.
2. Miss *America* is very *beautiful.*
3. Real *flowers* are *prettier than* plastic *flowers.*
4. *Where shall we eat?*
5. The *food* was really delicious.
6. *What will you have for breakfast?*
7. *I will go* to lunch early *today.*
8. *I will* make spaghetti *for dinner.*
9. *When will supper* be *ready?*
10. *That experience frightened* her.
11. *How could you sleep* so *long?*
12. The baby was so *sleepy* he *could not finish* his bottle.
13. Wear a *white* shirt.

14. *Our* flag is red, *white and* blue.
15. *Few* of *us will go.*
16. *A few* people are *coming this afternoon.*
17. *Several* people phoned *last night.*
18. *No one seems* to be *home.*

LESSON 19

1. The old *lady will sell* her *car.*
2. The corner *store is closing up.*
3. *Football* is a *rough* game.
4. *That workman looks rough.*
5. *What is your* phone *number?*
6. The snow *melted overnight.*
7. Sugar *dissolves in* water.
8. *I* never *saw you* so *angry.*
9. Please *mix* the paint.
10. *I* was lost *but not confused.*
11. The *new machine is not* difficult to use.
12. The desert has dry *soil.*
13. Children love to play *in* the *snow.*
14. *It rained* very hard *this morning.*
15. *We moved from* Baltimore *to* Washington.
16. *Place* the *book on my* desk.
17. *I don't remember where I put it.*
18. *What do you teach?*

LESSON 20

1. *We* are *happy since we* moved *to our new home.*
2. *Please don't* do *that.*
3. The *pleasure is all mine.*
4. *All* of *us enjoy* good *food.*
5. Do *you want sugar in your* coffee?
6. *This candy* is too *sweet for me.*
7. The baby had *on* a *cute* outfit.
8. The road was very *bad.*
9. *You* did a *good* job.
10. *Thank you* for *your* help.
11. *Your* perfume *smells* good.
12. His *parents* are *ashamed* of him.
13. He is too *shy* to *speak in* public.
14. *We will have* French *bread for* supper.

LESSON 21

1. The criminal was sent *to jail.*
2. *My father* is *in prison.*
3. Spring is a *wonderful time* of year.
4. *Sunday* is a *day* of rest.
5. *Monday* is wash *day.*
6. On *Tuesday, I* go shopping.

7. *Wednesday* is the middle of the week.
8. *I* play bridge on *Thursday.*
9. *Friday* is the start of the weekend.
10. *Saturday* is *my day* at the *beauty* shop.
11. How many *sons do you have?*
12. The fox is a wild *animal.*
13. *I* felt better *after seeing* the doctor.
14. The meeting was *already* in *progress.*
15. Let *me* know in *advance before you come.*
16. *What* is the *next lesson?*
17. The *baby* is very tiny.
18. *My sons don't look like brothers.*
19. *Your daughter* is very *pretty.*
20. *This place* is very *quiet.*
21. It was the *calm before* the storm.
22. *Be quiet* so *I can* study.
23. *We* hope to make *peace* soon.
24. *I admit that I* was wrong.
25. The *man confessed* to the crime.
26. *We* were *tired after that long* walk.
27. *Call his* attention to the mistake.
28. He *summoned me to* his office.
29. *I warned* him *about* the road.
30. *You will become* cold.
31. It is *getting* late.
32. The *stores* are *limiting* the *sale* of meat.
33. *I* am *satisfied with your work.*
34. *I* feel *relieved about that.*
35. *Autumn* will soon be *here.*
36. *We* climbed the *tree.*
37. Will *you* be *responsible for this?*
38. It was *not your fault.*
39. She *looks* very *young.*
40. *My* class is studying *parts* of the *body.*
41. *This* is *light* enough *for me* to *carry.*

LESSON 22

1. The *boy loves his* dog.
2. The Dolphins *beat* the Redskins.
3. The Pirates were *defeated.*
4. *I made* an *appointment with* the dean.
5. *Reserve* a table *for us, please.*
6. Do *you have reservations for* the show?
7. Baseball is popular *with* young *boys.*
8. The police will *guard that house.*
9. *Who will protect us?*
10. *Whom* did the lawyer *defend?*
11. East Germany has *no liberty.*
12. *For how long will you* be *free?*
13. *We must save his* life.
14. *What year* did *we* land *on* the moon?
15. *My father will* retire *next year.*
16. He *made* his *yearly* trip *home.*
17. *I like black coffee.*

18. Did *you make that* pie?
19. The Russians *exaggerate* a lot.
20. The *store advertised several* sales.
21. *Much propaganda comes from* Red China.

LESSON 23

1. *We visit* our *grandparents on Sunday.*
2. The storm *became worse.*
3. *Five multiplied* by *five* equals *twenty-five.*
4. *This lesson* is *hard.*
5. It is *difficult* to *drive on* icy roads.
6. *What* is *your problem?*
7. Pass the *salt, please.*
8. *Pepper makes me* sneeze.
9. *Who will supervise* the children?
10. *Can you take care of* my *pets while I* am away?
11. *Be careful when you cross* the street.
12. *You will lose your money if you* are *not careful.*
13. *You may keep* the *book.*
14. I must save money for my trip.
15. *Trains* are disappearing *from* the scene.
16. *May I borrow some paper?*
17. He applied *for* a *loan on* his *house.*
18. *I* am *very* tired.
19. *I don't like selfish* people.

LESSON 24

1. Many *goals* are *possible.*
2. *What* is *your objective in life?*
3. *This* can *go on forever.*
4. *In one month, I* learned *fingerspelling.*
5. *I* received a *monthly* bill *for that.*
6. *We* are *depending on you.*
7. The soldier was hurt in the *battle.*
8. A *war* is *going on in* Viet Nam.
9. Did *you suffer much pain?*
10. *I need some* aspirins *for my headache.*
11. A *toothache can* be *very painful.*
12. The little boy had a *stomachache.*
13. There are *various books on* the subject.
14. *I like variety in my* diet.
15. The temperature *varies* a great deal.
16. *Who* will *play opposite me?*
17. *He disagreed with his teacher.*
18. *He* has *made* many *enemies.*
19. The Rams and the Colts are *football opponents.*
20. *Life* is a *struggle.*
21. *Stop arguing!*
22. *Brothers* and *sisters often quarrel.*

LESSON 25

1. *Obey your mother* and *father.*
2. *Have you notified your school?*
3. *Inform me as soon as you can.*
4. *We didn't get that information.*
5. *My* pillow is so *soft.*
6. The *ground* is *very wet.*
7. The crops are *poor this* summer.
8. *It is obvious* he means *what he says.*
9. The sun is *very bright today.*
10. The *water* was quite *clear.*
11. The *colors* are *lighter in this* room.
12. *I accept* the prize *with much pleasure.*
13. Do *you give to* the United Fund?
14. *Where will you meet him?*
15. The Boy Scouts *congregated* at the park.
16. The *meeting* ended early.
17. Many *homes* were *destroyed in* the flood.
18. *You* are a *mean* person.

LESSON 26

1. His *death* was hard *for* her to *take* (accept).
2. How many people *died in* the accident?
3. *Please come home before dark.*
4. *What* is *better than* a *nice* warm *bath?*
5. *They sent their son* to college.
6. The young *boy* was *fired from* his job.
7. He is *separated from* his wife.
8. *What* do *you have planned for tomorrow?*
9. *Have you arranged for* the tour?
10. *I am preparing* a party *for 30* people.
11. *I* gave *my* grandson a *red boat.*
12. *Go* down *that road.*
13. The Mississippi is *our* largest *river.*
14. The *ocean* is rough today.
15. Use the *right method.*
16. Do *you know* of an *easy way* to do *this?*
17. The *street* is *in* need of repairs.
18. The *path* is lined *with flowers.*
19. Walk up the *narrow path.*
20. *I live on* a *wide street.*
21. *I* was *born* in the *middle* of the *night.*
22. The *birth* was a *difficult* one.
23. *Allow me* to *take you to* the train.
24. Will *you let me go to* church *with you?*
25. *This* is a *book* of *basic signs.*
26. *My house* is a split-level.
27. New York is a big *city.*
28. He moved *from* a small *town.*
29. The *community* parks are *beautiful.*
30. To *build* a house requires great skill.
31. *That building* is *new.*
32. *My professor* visited Russia last winter.

33. *Have you* taken *Russian?*
34. *I want to introduce you* to *my friend.*
35. *We* are *all invited* to the wedding.
36. *You* are *welcome* to *come* anytime.
37. It helps to practice *signs in* the *mirror.*
38. There is frost *on the window.*
39. I sent a *box* full of *clothes to* the Red Cross.
40. The couple *bought* a *10-room* house.
41. The *door to* the kitchen is *open.*
42. Were *you* late *for* the *meeting?*
43. *I have not yet eaten.*
44. The *boy* was sick *from too much candy.*
45. *Don't eat to excess.*

LESSON 27

1. She has a *heavy* heart.
2. *A* plus *B equals D* plus *E.*
3. *Some* meats *have less* fat *than others.*
4. The swelling was *decreasing.*
5. *We arrived* early *in* the *morning.*
6. The *college* is *close to center city.*
7. The firemen *approached* the *burning building.*
8. Do *you have proof?*
9. *We stopped near* Atlanta.
10. *Our neighbor* is deaf.
11. The little *boy* sat *between* his *mother* and *father.*
12. The *two girls* are *beside the tree.*
13. *Stop bothering me!*
14. *Your hands* are dirty.
15. His *father encouraged* him to *go to college.*
16. *I don't have* much *power in my* battery.
17. The *coffee* is *very strong.*
18. *My train* was *slow this morning.*
19. *You* must *improve your signs.*
20. The *old man's* health is *deteriorating.*
21. The *house* is *high* up *on* the hill.
22. The plane is flying *low.*
23. I *have finished this* assignment.
24. *This* is the *end* of the story.
25. The sculptor *has not completed* his *work.*
26. *What* were the *results?*
27. It was *kind of you* to *think of me.*
28. I *need* a *long* rest.
29. *No one worries about me.*
30. *What* is the *trouble with* the *car?*
31. *What* is *your problem?*
32. *Please pay attention* to the *speaker.*
33. I need a *quiet place* to *concentrate on my work.*
34. His remarks *embarrassed me.*
35. *Once in a while we blush.*
36. *My brother* is a *head* taller *than my sister.*

37. Do *you like* to be *in* the *center* of *things?*
38. *I* am in the *middle* of *making breakfast.*
39. The heater is *in* the *middle* of the *room.*
40. He has *not yet* learned to *divide.*
41. *What* is the *cause* of his *death?*

LESSON 28

1. *I felt sick from* the hot dogs.
2. *My grandmother* is *feeling better now.*
3. *I* have *no sympathy for* him.
4. It is a *pity you can't go.*
5. He is *all heart.*
6. Lemonade *tastes good on* a *hot day.*
7. The *food* was *delicious.*
8. *You must* be *very smart.*
9. The dog *does clever* tricks.
10. *I felt* so *dirty after playing* tennis.
11. *Pigs eat* garbage.
12. *What makes you think* she *likes* him?
13. *I don't like* her.
14. *What* was so *interesting about* it?
15. The *life* of *Jesus* is *discussed in* the *New* Testament.
16. *Do you* read the *Bible?*
17. The home run was a real *thrill.*
18. The *excitement* of the crowd finally died down.
19. He is a *very emotional man.*
20. *I hate* to *go* to the *hospital.*
21. *Buy* a *new dictionary.*

LESSON 29

1. *How odd that* she had *not heard about* it.
2. There was a *strange man in* the *neighborhood.*
3. He *gave us* a *most peculiar look.*
4. *My son* went *hunting for* deer.
5. The police are *searching for* the *lost boy.*
6. *Everyone* is *looking for you.*
7. Did *you hear that scream?*
8. *You don't* have to *shout!*
9. Did *you drink all that* beer?
10. I *wish you* would *stop complaining.*
11. *You must* be *hungry after all that work.*
12. *When* will *you marry him?*
13. *This* is *her third marriage.*
14. They *announced* their *engagement.*
15. It was a *beautiful wedding.*
16. *Some marriages end in divorce.*
17. *What does your husband do?*
18. His *wife works part time.*
19. *No one* was *listening* to her *anyway.*

20. The *class* was *made up* of *two groups.*
21. A *group* of *us* are going *to* the beach.
22. The young *man* is *looking for action.*
23. *How can* these *activities* help *us?*
24. *What* do *you* want to *do?*
25. The *coffee* had *frozen.*

LESSON 30

1. Northern *Italy* is *very beautiful.*
2. *Italian food* is *delicious.*
3. Do *you* belong to the *Catholic* Church?
4. The *institution* of the family is important.
5. There is a *residential school for* the deaf *in most* states.
6. The producer *has some good ideas for* the *play.*
7. *Can you imagine her becoming* an actress?
8. He is the *jealous* type.
9. *Why* are *you* so *envious?*
10. Do *you dream often?*
11. *I* would *like* to *visit Japan some day.*
12. The *Japanese language* is *very difficult.*
13. *China* is a *very* large country.
14. The *Chinese* are *hard-working* people.
15. John was *last in* the race.
16. *This* is *my final* race.

LESSON 31

1. *He* is certainly *not lazy.*
2. *I sometimes loaf around* the *house.*
3. *I will have two weeks' vacation.*
4. The secretary *retired after 25 years with* the company.
5. *I want* to *see* him *in person.*
6. *Have you seen this individual before?*
7. How many *people* are *going on* the picnic?
8. *My* boss *has* an *appointment with his doctor this morning.*
9. Dr. Robinson is a *psychiatrist.*
10. The *nurse* assisted *in* the *operation.*
11. A *large house* is *hard* to *clean.*
12. *It* was *not* as *big* as *I thought it* was.
13. *How big* was the plane?
14. *He* was a *small man.*
15. *May I* have *that little* piece of cake?
16. The *dress* is a *perfect* fit.
17. *Exactly how* do *you* like *your egg?*
18. *This is precisely* the *way I* like *it.*
19. Do *I* have *permission to go?*
20. *It* was a *privilege* to *hear* him *speak.*
21. *I thought* the *place* was *very pretty.*
22. There is a *new position in* the company.
23. Do *you know that area?*

114

LESSON 32

1. The grass is *green now.*
2. *In* October, the leaves *become brown.*
3. *Red* is *my* favorite *color.*
4. *Babies* are usually *born with blue* eyes.
5. The *house* has *yellow doors* and *windows.*
6. *Not all* grapes are *purple.*
7. *See that orange* sunset.
8. *Have you* ever *seen a pink* Cadillac?
9. John wore a *gray* business suit.
10. Do *you work in Washington, D.C.?*
11. Washington is the *"father* of *our* country."
12. The *water* was *very cold.*
13. French *people drink wine with all* their meals.
14. *Vinegar goes* well *with* spinach.
15. It is an *expensive restaurant.*
16. *Most women* are *frightened* of *rats.*
17. The cat *tried* to catch the *mouse.*
18. *People* had *much respect for* him.
19. He was an *honor* student.
20. *When* will *you* be *ready?*
21. *Some words* sound *alike.*
22. The *teacher gave her students* a *vocabulary* test.
23. The *world* is *getting smaller.*

LESSON 33

1. Many *people in* the United States are *deaf.*
2. *We hope to go* to Europe *someday.*
3. *When shall I expect you to come?*
4. *We praised them for doing what they* did.
5. *I congratulated* the *minister on* his *interesting sermon.*
6. A *promise* is a *promise!*
7. He *disappeared right after lunch.*
8. Suddenly he *appeared.*
9. They *tried to escape from jail.*
10. *Can you begin your job tomorrow?*
11. *I could not start my car.*
12. He *swallowed the whole thing.*
13. Are *you thirsty?*
14. Read the story, *then answer* the questions.
15. *You* must rest *for a week.*
16. The *maid comes to clean for us weekly.*
17. *Next week we leave for* Hawaii.
18. *Our* salesman was *out of town last week.*
19. *We* were *among* the first to *arrive.*
20. *Show me the way to go* home.
21. *I will demonstrate* the *new gadget.*
22. He *illustrated* the *meaning of* the *word.*
23. *For example, how do you feel about oralism?*
24. *Please pay your debts as soon as possible.*

25. *I saw* the *play once before.*
26. *Sometimes I* jog *around* the block.
27. *Occasionally, I* go *to* New York *for some shopping.*
28. James *has* a lot of *debts.*
29. *What* do *we owe for* the repairs?
30. History is *my major.*
31. His *specialty* is *Italian* poetry.
32. *What* was his *line of work (occupation)?*
33. *Most professionals* attend the seminars.
34. He is the best *in* his *field!*
35. *Please discuss that* subject *carefully.*
36. The *debate* required *2-1/2 hours.*
37. John had a *big argument with* his *wife.*
38. The track *meet* was *cancelled because* of rain.
39. *I criticized him for not coming to* the *meeting.*
40. The *mother corrected* her child *on* his *manners.*
41. He is *very tall for* his *age.*
42. *Meet me on* the *northeast* corner of the block.
43. Do *you believe everything you hear?*
44. *We have faith you will succeed.*

LESSON 34

1. *I guess I* should *write to my sister.*
2. The *old ladies missed* the bus.
3. The *President* is at Camp David *today.*
4. He is the *superintendent* of a *school for* the *deaf.*
5. The writer is *trying* to *condense his* novel.
6. *How* do *you abbreviate that word?*
7. *We* are *summarizing several books.*
8. *Drink your milk!*
9. There *will always* be an *England.*
10. The *English language* is *very* widespread.
11. *To which church* do *you* belong?
12. The Hebrew *temple* is *very old.*
13. The *police* are *here* to *ask some questions.*
14. *May I have a glass of water please?*
15. *May I have a cup* of tea?
16. There are at least *four* major *religions.*
17. *How old* is *your grandmother?*
18. Her *age shows.*
19. *Many* of *my friends* are *Jewish.*
20. Daisies *grow on my* lawn.
21. Birds fly north *in* the *spring.*

LESSON 35

1. *Let me show you some pictures* of *our* trip.
2. He is *too fat.*
3. *We cannot use up everything* at *once.*

4. *Our* gasoline supply is *almost exhausted (depleted).*
5. The newsboy is *earning money for college.*
6. He *has a large income from* stock.
7. *Subtract* 7 from 13.
8. *Remove your coat.*
9. Do *you* use *cream in your coffee?*
10. *My son likes* to read sports *magazines.*
11. *Give me that new booklet.*
12. *I* read a *pamphlet on* insurance *yesterday.*
13. *Count* the *number* of votes, please.
14. These *numbers don't add up right.*
15. *Meat* has *become very expensive.*
16. It is *not difficult* to *make gravy.*
17. The fried chicken was *too greasy for me.*
18. The soldiers *felt they did their duty.*
19. Lincoln was a *very honest man.*
20. Did *you register for* the *course?*
21. *More than thirty people signed* the petition.
22. Do *you* have a neat *signature?*
23. *We* must *find* directions *to the place.*
24. Columbus *discovered America.*
25. *Pick up* the *broken* glass.
26. *Pick out* the *color you want*
27. *What* was *your selection for dinner?*
28. *His choice of school* was excellent.
29. Did *you print that money yourself?*
30. *From which college* did he *graduate?*
31. It was a *beautiful* gold *certificate.*

LESSON 36

1. *Some men* are *better cooks than their wives.*
2. *It* is *best that you take a short vacation.*
3. *His* manners *impressed me very much.*
4. *Certain things must* be *emphasized.*
5. *We must establish a good* relationship *with* the students.
6. *Set up* the tent.
7. *I saw your aunt* at the store.
8. The *letter had no stamp on it.*
9. Has the *mail come in yet?*
10. *Go to* the Post Office *for some stamps.*
11. *Please practice your* piano *lesson.*
12. The soldiers were *trained for* the battlefront.
13. The guide *led us through* the cave.
14. *Some people need* to be *guided.*
15. *He* was the *first one into* the pool.
16. *Some people have more ability than others.*
17. To be a surgeon, *you must have much skill.*
18. Robin Hood was an *expert* marksman.
19. *Do not forget to buy some milk on your way home.*
20. *My professor* is *becoming very forgetful.*

LESSON 37

1. It's *none of your business.*
2. He was *very busy.*
3. *I* must *study in a quiet room.*
4. *Obey* the *rules of your* dormitory.
5. The *Constitution* of the U.S. is an *interesting* document.
6. *We must follow* the *law as much as we can.*
7. *That* is *forbidden by the Constitution.*
8. *It* was *against his principles to do that.*
9. Are *you for or against this law?*
10. *I oppose* the amendment.
11. *Help me remove* the tire.
12. Do *you think we* should *aid* Israel?
13. *We appreciate your assistance.*
14. *Can we count on your support?*
15. The *house* is *built on a new foundation.*
16. *We met his assistant in* the laboratory.
17. *Every morning I hear* the birds *sing.*
18. *We can make beautiful music together.*
19. The *poetry* of Yeats is *well known.*
20. A *friend of mine* is *a song* writer.
21. *We* went to a *dance last night.*
22. *We gave* a surprise *party for* the *new* couple.
23. *Can you come* back *later, please?*
24. The T.V. repairman *will come after a while.*
25. The dentist will *see you in a minute.*
26. An *hour's* swim is *long enough.*
27. *Please give me enough time to get* there.
28. There is *plenty* of ice cream *for all.*
29. *Fill the glass with milk.*
30. He was *fully* conscious *during the operation.*
31. *I am completely* at a loss for words.
32. *Draw me* a map of the *way to your place.*
33. Are *you very good in Art class?*
34. *My* dressmaker *designs beautiful clothes.*
35. *She painted a portrait of her daughter.*
36. *I had my house painted* in *white.*
37. *That big lunch* made *me full.*

LESSON 38

1. *French* chefs are *very much in* demand.
2. *France* is an *exciting* country.
3. She *has 44 cats.*
4. *Where is your college spirit?*
5. *Suffering* is *good for* the *soul.*
6. He was *dressed as a ghost on* Halloween.
7. *Why is this course so important?*
8. *What is this land worth?*
9. *Most people value* health *above wealth.*
10. The *workers* are *required to join* the union.
11. Do *you* belong to that *new* country *club?*
12. *Our workers* are *cooperating in a car* pool.

13. Does *this relate* to *your work?*
14. *Will you please explain what happened?*
15. The *woman* is *trying* to *describe* the thief.
16. *I will manage* the *shop while you* are *gone.*
17. He *has control* of the union.
18. *We need* a *new director.*
19. A *glass* of iced *tea* is *very* refreshing.
20. I saw an *awful* accident *on* the highway.
21. The *book* was *terrible* in *places.*
22. *Instead of* staying *home, we* went *to* a movie.
23. The *meeting* was *postponed.*
24. *Some people* write *very lengthy sentences.*
25. *My sister can speak five languages.*
26. His *grammar* was *poor.*
27. Would *you like* to "hear" a *story in sign language?*
28. *All* of *us except* Mike *went to* the *party.*
29. It was an *exceptional* novel.
30. *This* is a *special day.*
31. The *men volunteered* to fight the *fire.*
32. *Is* he a *candidate for that job?*
33. The *manager applied for* a transfer.
34. *This man has my vote.*
35. *We elected him president* of the club.
36. I am *curious about our new neighbors.*
37. *We will decide about that later.*
38. *Have you determined* the penalty?
39. He *had to go to court to pay* his *fines.*
40. She *shows very good judgment.*
41. The conductor is a *good judge* of *music.*

LESSON 39

1. The *punishment* should fit the crime.
2. *Why* are *you penalizing* him *for* her *mistake?*
3. The *new tax will* be *4* percent.
4. *How much* did *it cost you* to fly round trip?
5. *May I charge this to my* account?
6. *I demand* a *new* roof *for my house.*
7. *It takes* an *hour for my* hair to dry.
8. *This job requires* a *skillful* operator.
9. *I forgot my key* to *the house.*
10. *Make sure you lock* the *door.*
11. *He means business!*
12. *She did that on purpose.*
13. *My son intends to buy* a boat.
14. The *new bridge* is *three* miles *long.*
15. *Where* do *I stand with you?*
16. *Arise and walk!*
17. *Kneel and pray.*
18. The *boy fell off his bibyble.*
19. *I will lie down and* take a nap.
20. He *failed* to *keep his promise.*
21. The *old man slipped on* the ice.
22. *Can you hop 50* yards?

23. *How* far *can you jump?*
24. It is *only* a *short walk to my* office.
25. *He* is the *best runner on* the team.

LESSON 40

1. *My* battery is *weak.*
2. *What* are *you learning in that course?*
3. *Education helps you succeed in life.*
4. *I have three new students in my class.*
5. *May I have* a *copy* of the *letter?*
6. The *comedian* is *good* at *imitating famous people.*
7. *I* received a *telegram this morning.*
8. His *wire reached me* in Paris.
9. Do *you have any* cough *medicine?*
10. *I plan* to *write* a *letter to* the *President.*
11. Do *you have* a *red pencil that I can borrow?*
12. *I read "A Tale of Two Cities" twice.*
13. His *secretary made* notes of the *meeting.*
14. *That* was an *X*-rated *movie.*

LESSON 41

1. *It* was *dumb of me to leave my keys in* the *car.*
2. *Don't give up* so *easily.*
3. *Japan surrendered* in August *1945.*
4. *I thrill* at *your touch!*
5. *I will contact you as* soon *as I hear from* him.
6. He *put poison in* her *tea.*
7. Did *you win in* the golf tournament?
8. *My parents celebrated their 50*th *wedding anniversary.*
9. *It* was an *important victory.*
10. There *is* a *good German restaurant in* town.
11. The *President* was *in Germany last spring.*
12. The *exact time* is *given on* radio *and* T.V.
13. *That happened* a *long time ago.*
14. He *counselled me* to *take this course.*
15. The *doctor advised me* to rest *more.*
16. He is a *bad influence.*
17. Did *you take* her *to* the *dance?*
18. The *faculty has taken up* the issue.
19. Are *you taking* biology *this* semester?
20. *He dropped this* course because he *was taking too many.*
21. Do *you like* boiled *potatoes?*
22. *I will visit Ireland this summer.*
23. *Many people of Irish* descent *live in* Boston.
24. He *travels all over* the *world.*
25. *Where* did *you get that book?*
26. *I got* the *book* at the public library.
27. Have *you received any calls from* him?

28. *Try* to *catch* the *first train.*
29. The *earth* is a *very small* planet.
30. Do *you know much about* the *geography* of the U.S.?
31. The *house* had a *vacant look about* it.
32. The swimming pool was *empty.*
33. The *rooms* are *bare in* the *old house.*
34. The *boys* are swimming *nude in* the creek.
35. Did *you* see the *blank look on his face?*
36. *Over* the *years,* he had *become bald.*
37. *Yes, we* will *take you to* the airport.
38. The airlines *will go on strike starting* at *midnight.*
39. The *rebellion* was quieted.
40. *Ireland* is *in revolt.*

LESSON 42

1. He *made* a *funny face.*
2. *We* had *fun* at the *party.*
3. *Please hurry and drive us to* the *hospital.*
4. The *father told* a *short story before putting* the *children* to bed.
5. *Our President* is *now in* the *hospital.*
6. The *nurse* is *in* the *infirmary.*
7. *Doctors* are *busy visiting their patients.*
8. *I quit* smoking *two years ago.*
9. *Can we participate?*
10. *If we can join, we will.*
11. *Put butter on* the *bread.*
12. *How would you like your eggs for breakfast?*
13. *I* must *watch my weight.*
14. *2000 pounds equals one ton.*
15. *I prefer* to *do it myself.*
16. *Increase* the *number by 10 and subtract 3.*
17. *What is your middle name?*
18. *We call our* dog "Bubba."
19. *What is* the *title of that book?*
20. *You can quote me.*
21. *Where* do *you sit in class?*
22. *That* is *not* a *very good seat.*
23. *I love my comfortable chair.*
24. *History* is an *interesting subject* (course).
25. *How do you use this machine?*
26. She *wears nice clothes.*

LESSON 43

1. *We vacationed on* the southern coast of Spain.
2. *My daughter speaks Spanish.*
3. *We must learn other languages.*
4. *I need* a pair of *new shoes.*
5. *You ought* to *pay* her a *visit.*

6. *We really should stop for* a *while.*
7. *I have to hurry now but I will see you later.*
8. The *boys damaged my car* by *playing* ball *near it.*
9. The *heavy rain ruined* his *crops.*
10. He is *always teasing the girls.*
11. *Have you taken* the chemistry *test* yet?
12. *Don't ask me about* him.
13. Do *you have* a *question?*
14. The *ground* is *very dry.*
15. The *lecture* was *very dull (boring).*
16. The *new shoe* styles are *ugly.*
17. It has been a *hot, dry summer.*
18. *I think* she *made* a *wise decision.*
19. *I changed my mind.*
20. *I suspected something* was *wrong.*
21. Did *you notice* her *new* fur *coat?*
22. *What* state is *your friend from?*
23. *All my relatives* are *dead.*
24. *Physics* is a *hard subject.*
25. The *electricity* went off *during* the storm.

LESSON 44

1. *America* is a *beautiful country.*
2. *My son* cut *himself while shaving.*
3. He was *wrong about* the *time* of the *meeting.*
4. She *made* a *mistake in* typing the *letter.*
5. He *admitted that* it was an *error.*
6. He is *still trying* to repair the *car.*
7. *Measure* the *length* of the *box.*
8. *Please stay for* a *while longer.*
9. *I hope my son continues with* his *studies.*
10. His *money could not last very long.*
11. It was *silly* of him to show off.
12. *Only* a *fool* would swim *that* far *out.*
13. It was *ridiculous* of him to *stay* so *long in* the *hot* sun.
14. *My new telephone* is *pink.*
15. Will *you please make* a *telephone call for me?*
16. The *baby loves* to *play with* his *toys.*
17. *Let's go* to a *party.*

LESSON 45

1. The 747 *airplane* is *huge.*
2. *More people* are *flying* these *days.*
3. Athens is the *capital of Greece.*
4. *My son* has *joined* a *Greek-letter* fraternity.
5. *Gallaudet College* has *deaf students from all over the world.*
6. *I need glasses now for reading.*
7. He *got* a *ticket for* speeding.
8. *I need a little bit more sugar in my tea.*

9. *How fast* was *that car going?*
10. *Quickly, hide* the *box before* he *comes.*
11. *We have many friends.*
12. *How much bread* do *you want?*
13. *How many* miles is it *to* Baltimore?
14. *Where* did *you hide* the cookies?
15. *Have you heard* the *latest gossip?*
16. *Both* of *us* were *very tired.*
17. He *got* his *revenge in* a *funny way.*
18. *Change* the *baby's* diaper.
19. *Can you reverse* interpret?
20. Were *you surprised to see* him?
21. *How long have you* been *awake?*
22. *Please wake me up* at 6 *o'clock.*

MANUAL COMMUNICATION BIBLIOGRAPHY

(Revised 1973 by Thomas Tyberg, Teacher,
New York School for the Deaf, White Plains)

The following bibliography is a compilation of the more recent works published relevant to manual communication. There are a variety of publications listed, some of which will interest teachers and students of fingerspelling and signs; others which will be of interest primarily to researchers. Entries with older copyrights, and those which are now out of print are included as research sources.

To enable readers to utilize this bibliography more effectively, each entry is preceded by a symbol (D, R, T, X, or *). The symbols designate whether the entry is a dictionary (D), a research source (R), a teaching resource (T), a text (X), or a specialized manual (*).

Prices and sources of texts are listed on the pages immediately following the bibliographical entries.

T   1.   Babbini, Barbara E. *Manual Communication: A Course of Study Outline for Instructors.* Urbana, Illinois: University Press, 1973.

X   2.   Babbini, Barbara E. *Manual Communication: A Course of Study Outline for Students.* Urbana, Illinois: University Press, 1973.

R   3.   Baynes, H. L. *Basic Signs.* (Out of print. One pamphlet in Gallaudet College Library.)

R   4.   Becker, Valentine A. *Underwater Sign Language.* (Catalog No. 1919, U.S. Divers Corps. Write to the author, Supervisor of Physically Handicapped, Public School System, San Francisco, California.)

D   5.   Benson, Elizabeth. *Sign Language.* St. Paul, Minnesota: St. Paul Technical Vocational Institute, 1964.

D   6.   Bornstein, Harry, Lillian Hamilton, Barbara Kannapell, Howard Roy and Karen Saulnier. *Basic Pre-school Signed-English Dictionary.* Washington, D. C.: Gallaudet College Press, 1973.

D   7.   Bornstein, Harry, Lillian Hamilton and Barbara Kannapell. *Signs for Instructional Purposes.* Washington, D. C.: Gallaudet College Press, 1969.

D   8.   Casterline, Dorothy, Carl C. Croneberg and William C. Stokoe, Jr. *A Dictionary of American Sign Language on Linguistic Principles.* Washington, D.C., Gallaudet College Press, 1965.

D/R   9.   Cissna, Roy. *Basic Sign Language.* Jefferson City, Missouri: Missouri Baptist Convention, 1963. (Out of print)

R/*   10.   Cokely, Dennis R. and Rev. Rudolph Gawlik. *Options—A Position Paper on the Relationship Between Manual English and Sign.* Washington, D. C.: Kendall Demonstration Elementary School for the Deaf, 1973. (Reprinted in the Deaf American, May 1973, limited copies available from authors.)

D   11.   Davis, Anne. *The Language of Signs.* New York: Executive Council of the Episcopal Church, 1966.

*   12.   Delaney, Theo and C. Bailey. *Sing Unto the Lord: A Hymnal for the Deaf.* (Hymns translated into signs.) Ephphetha Conference of Lutheran Pastors for the Deaf, 1959.

R/X   13.   Falberg, Roger M. *The Language of Silence.* Wichita, Kansas: Wichita Social Services for the Deaf, 1963.

X   14.   Fant, Louie J. *Ameslan: An Introduction to American Sign Language.* Silver Spring, Maryland: National Association of the Deaf, 1972.

T   15.   Fant, Louie J. *Ameslan: An Introduction to American Sign Language-Teacher's Guide.* Silver Spring, Maryland: National Association of the Deaf, 1972.

D/T   16.   Fant, Louie J. *Say It With Hands.* Washington, D. C.: American Annals of the Deaf, Gallaudet College, 1964.

R   17.   Fauth, Bette La Verne and Warren Wesley Fauth. "A Study of Proceedings of the Convention of American Instructors of the Deaf, 1850-1949, IV," Chapter XIII, "The Manual Alphabet," *American Annals of the Deaf,* 196:292-296, March, 1951. (Bibliography included)

R   18.   Fauth, Bette La Verne and Warren Wesley Fauth. "Sign Language," *American Annals of the Deaf,* 100:253-263, March, 1955.

R   19.   Geylman, I. "The Sign Language and Hand Alphabet of Deaf Mutes," *Proceedings of the Workshop on Interpreting for the Deaf.* Muncie, Indiana: Ball State Teachers College, 1964, pp. 62-90.

T   20.   Guillory, LaVera M. *Expressive and Receptive Fingerspelling for Hearing Adults.* Baton Rouge, Louisiana: Claitor's Book Store, 1966.

D   21.   Gustason, Gerilee, Donna Pfetzing and Ester Zawolkow. *Signing Exact English. Seeing Instead of Hearing.* Rossmoor, California: Modern Sign Press, 1972

D   22.   Higgins, Daniel, C.S.S.R. *How to Talk to the Deaf.* Newark, New Jersey: Mount Carmel Guild, Archdiocese of Newark, 1959.

D   23.   Hoemann, Harry W., Ed. *Improved Techniques of Communication: A Training Manual for Use With Severely Handicapped Deaf Clients.* Bowling Green State University, 1970.

T   24.   Jordan, Florence. *Lesson Outlines for Teaching and the Study of Dactylology.* Hampton, Virginia.

*   26.   Landes, Robert M. *Approaches: A Digest of Methods in Learning the Language of Signs.* Richmond, Virginia, 1968.

D/R   27.   Long, J. Schuyler. *The Sign Language: A Manual of Signs.* Washington, D. C.: Gallaudet College, 1962. (Out of print)

T/X   28.   Madsen, Willard J. *Conversational Sign Language II: An Intermediate-Advanced Manual.* Washington, D. C.: Gallaudet College, 1972.

R   29.   Michaels, J. W. *A Handbook of the Sign Language.* Atlanta, Georgia: Home Mission Board, Southern Baptist Convention, 1923. (Out of print)

T/X   30.   Myers, Lowell L. *The Law and the Deaf.* (For information write to Dr. Boyce R. Williams, Director, Communication Disorders Branch, Rehabilitation Services Administration, Department of Health, Education, and Welfare, Washington, D. C. 20201.)

D/T/X 31. O'Rourke, Terrence J., *A Basic Course in Manual Communication.* (Revised edition) Silver Spring, Maryland: National Association of the Deaf, 1973.

R/* 32. O'Rourke, Terrence, J., Ed. *Psycholinguistics and Total Communication: The State of the Art.* Washington, D. C.: The American Annals of the Deaf, 1972.

R 33. Peet, Elizabeth. "The Philology of the Sign Language," *Buff and Blue.* Gallaudet College, March, 1921. (Out of print)

T/* 34. Quigley, S. P., Ed. *Interpreting for Deaf People.* Workshop report. U.S. Department of Health, Education, and Welfare, Washington, D. C. 20201, 1965.

R 35. Rand, Lawrence W. *An Annotated Bibliography of the Sign Language of the Deaf.* Seattle, Washington: University of Washington, 1962. (Unpublished M.A. Thesis)

D/X 36. Riekehof, Lottie L. *Talk to the Deaf.* Springfield, Missouri: Gospel Publishing House, 1963.

D/R 37. Roth, Stanley D. *A Basic Book of Signs Used by the Deaf.* Fulton, Missouri: Missouri School for the Deaf, 1948. (Out of print)

D 38. Sanders, Josef I., Ed. *The ABC's of Sign Language.* Tulsa, Oklahoma: Manca Press, 1968.

T/* 39. Schein, Jerome D., Martin L. A. Sternberg and Carol C. Tipton. *Interpreter Training: A Curriculum Guide,* New York: Deafness Research and Training Center, New York University, 1973.

R 40. Siger, Leonard C. "Gestures, the Language of Signs, and Human Communication," *American Annals of the Deaf,* 113:11-28, January, 1968.

R 41. Smith, Jess M. *Workshop on Interpreting for the Deaf.* Department of Health, Education and Welfare, VRA Grant #460-T-64, 1964. (Out of print)

D/X 42. Springer, C. S., C.S.S.R. *Talking With the Deaf.* Baton Rouge, Louisiana: Redemptorist Fathers, 1961.

R 43. Stokoe, W. C. *Sign Language Structure: An Outline of the Visual Communication Systems of the American Deaf.* Buffalo, New York: University of Buffalo, 1960.

R 44. Stokoe, William C. *The Study of Sign Language.* Silver Spring, Maryland: National Association of the Deaf (revised edition), 1971. (No longer in print; original available from ERIC Document Reproduction Center.)

T/R/* 45. Taylor, Lucile N., Ed. *Proceedings of the Registry of Interpreters for the Deaf: Workshop II.* Mimeographed. (Write to editor, Wisconsin School for the Deaf, Delavan, Wisconsin 53115.)

D/X 46. Washington State School for the Deaf. *An Introduction to Manual English.* Vancouver, Washington: Washington State School for the Deaf, 1972.

D/X 47. Watson, David. *Talk With Your Hands.* Menasha, Wisconsin: George Banta Publishing Company, 1963.

D/X 48. Watson, David. *Talk With Your Hands, Volumes I and II.* Menasha, Wisconsin: George Banta Publishing Company, 1973.

R   49.   Wisher, Peter R. *Use of the Sign Language in Underwater Communication.* Washington, D. C.: Lithography by Gallaudet College.

The following indexes to the *American Annals of the Deaf* indicate additional references to articles in the *Annals* that deal with sign language. The page numbers given refer to the pages in the indexes on which these articles are listed.

Index No.	Page No.	Index No.	Page No.
I	40-45	VI	433
II	85-87	VII	537-538
III	86	VIII	545
IV	75	IX	404
V	78		

Index Number 10 has not yet been published. The Volume numbers and pagination for articles on manual communication which have appeared in the *Annals* since 1956 are listed below.

Volume No.	Page No.	Volume No.	Page No.
101	245-254	111	452-460
103	264-282		499-504
	524-525		557-565
104	232-240	113	11-28
105	232-237		29-41
	434	117	20-24
106	11-28		27-33
109	364-366		403-411
110	483-485	118	454-463
	585		

TEXT SOURCES AND PRICES: *(Postage not included.)*

Available from:
National Association of the Deaf, 814 Thayer Avenue, Silver Spring, Maryland 20910
or
Gallaudet College Bookstore, 7th and Florida Avenue, N.E., Washington, D.C. 20002

Available from:
International Association of Parents of the Deaf, 814 Thayer Avenue, Silver Spring, Maryland 20910

Available from Gallaudet College Bookstore:
    Bornstein, et al., Instr.
    Bornstein, et al., Dict.
    Casterline, et al.
    Davis
    Falberg
    Springer
    Stokoe
    Children's Storybooks in Signed English
    Children's Posters in Signed English

Private Sources:
Babbini -
                University of Illinois
                University Press
                Urbana, Illinois 61801

Delaney -
                Board of Missions
                The Lutheran Church
                Missouri Synod
                210 North Broadway
                St. Louis, Missouri 63102

Falberg -
                Deaf and Hard of Hearing Counseling Service, Inc.
                1648 East Central
                Wichita, Kansas 67214

Higgins -   Archdiocesan Audio-Visual Department
                Mount Carmel Guild
                603 Mulberry Street
                Newark, New Jersey 07114

Jordan -
                75 Broden Lane
                Hampton, Virginia 23366

Kosche -   Write to author
                116 Walnut Street
                Delavan, Wisconsin 53115

Landes -
                Baptist Book Store #4478
                115 East Grace Street
                Richmond, Virginia 23219

Quigley -   Registry of Interpreters for the Deaf
                P.O. Box 1339
                Washington, D.C. 20013
                        or
                Boyce R. Williams, Director
                Office of Deafness and Communicative Disorders
                Rehabilitation Services Administration
                H E W South Building 3414
                Washington, D.C. 20201

Sanders -
                Manca Press
                Tulsa, Oklahoma

125

Springer -
                Redemptorist Fathers
                5354 Plank Road
                Baton Rouge, Louisiana 70805

Washington -
                Washington State School for the Deaf
                P.O. Box 2036
                Vancouver, Washington 98661

Wisher -
                Write to author
                Department of Physical Education
                Gallaudet College
                7th and Florida Avenue, N.E.
                Washington, D.C. 20002

A SELECTED ANNOTATED BIBLIOGRAPHY OF
BOOKS, FILMS AND TEACHING MEDIA
ON SIGN LANGUAGE

Revised 1973 by Thomas Tyberg, Teacher, New York School for the Deaf, White Plains.

The reviews in *Interpreting for Deaf People* were presented under the heading "Annotated Bibliography of Books and Films on Sign Language." These reviews were prepared by the participants in the workshop on interpreting held at the Governor Baxter State School for the Deaf, Portland, Maine, July 7-27, 1965. All of the participants were supplied with a set of the books several weeks prior to the time the workshop was held. This allowed each person to spend some time reviewing the books before going to Maine. Each book was assigned to two participants for review. These persons prepared and distributed a written review to the other members of the workshop. At a general meeting, comments and suggestions were made concerning the reviews which usually led to revisions of the original reviews. The reviews then were edited for presentation in an appendix.

Since the publication of the manual *Interpreting for Deaf People* in 1965, a number of new books and other materials on fingerspelling and the language of signs have appeared in the United States. Only those books with copyrights dating from 1966 have been annotated for inclusion in this revision. Asterisks (*) precede the entries annotated for the revision, and will permit readers to locate the new entires more readily.

This second revision was undertaken by the Communicative Skills Program of the National Association of the Deaf.

*1. Babbini, Barbara E. *Manual Communication: A Course of Study Outline for Instructors.* Urbana, Illinois: University Press, 1971.

This revision of the previous title, *An Introductory Course in Manual Communication: Fingerspelling and the Language of Signs*, is a very good manual for use by teachers as an outline and source of information for teaching sign language and fingerspelling. The manual is divided into two parts.

Part I includes general information for the teacher on signing and fingerspelling, such as points on receptive and expressive skills. Also, the teacher is provided with information on procedures and techniques that may be utilized with the student text (see next entry) and lesson plans. An extensive unit on the use of videotape, television and other media is also contained within the manual.

The second part is the actual course outline with lesson plans. There are two sections to this part, a Beginning section and an Intermediate section. In the Beginning section are two lessons on fingerspelling, one on numbers, and a review lesson. The remainder of the section is composed of 10 lessons on learning new signs. Signs in the manual are grouped to express related ideas, thus providing for continuity and expansion. The teaching lessons follow a similar format, with easy to follow general instructions, a list of materials required, a complete lesson plan outline, practice materials, and a vocabulary list.

The Intermediate section continues to expand vocabulary and builds on the Beginning section. Eleven lessons with similar format to the Beginning section, minus the general instructions, present additional signs and practice. A total of about 600 signs is presented in both the Beginning and Intermediate sections.

The Appendix includes a variety of materials: 1) a master vocabulary list, 2) student progress charts, 3) a student roster, 4) grade sheets, and 5) an annotated bibliography.

Class sessions are expected to be about 2-3 hours, with drills and other activities, twice a week for 11 weeks. The instructor utilizing the outline is also assumed to have a good working knowledge of signs. A student manual has also been prepared to accompany the manual.

*2. Babbini, Barbara E. *Manual Communication: A Course of Study Outline for Students.* Urbana, Illinois: University Press, 1971.

This manual is a student's workbook designed to be used in classes taught by instructors using the aforementioned manual, and the material therein is coordinated with the lesson plans given. Included are a brief history of the language of signs; Do's and Don'ts in the Language of Signs and Fingerspelling; word-descriptions of the signs given in each lesson; practice words, numbers and sentences for each lesson; homework assignments, and an Appendix which includes a bibliography of books and articles on the language of signs, fingerspelling and deafness in general. Also included in the Appendix are charts upon which students can record grades received on tests and assignments.

Illustrations include the drawings of the handshapes of the Manual Alphabet; the numbers from 1 to 10; and the fundamental Hand-Positions upon which the word-descriptions of the signs are based. (The latter illustration was prepared for the author's original Course of Study Outline by David O. Watson in 1965 and is retained herein.)

3. Benson, Elizabeth. *Sign Language.* St. Paul, Minnesota: St. Paul Area Technical Vocational Institute, 196-

St. Paul Area Technical Vocational Institute has published *Sign Language*, a manual of Dr. Elizabeth Benson's materials for the teaching of the language of signs. Previously unpublished, these materials were collated and used by the author in classes at Gallaudet College under the title, "Suggestions Relative to the Mastery of Signs."

The 590 signs described in verbal notations constitute a basic sign language vocabulary, the unique factor being Dr. Benson's original arrangement of the vocabulary into 19 discrete categories under such headings as "Animals," "Opposites," "Recreation," "Time," and "Verbs."

Because verbal descriptions are not accurate, students must be shown the proper signs by a competent teacher. Then, this manual becomes appropriate for review. Thirty-one pages are devoted to descriptions of signs that are presented in the illustrated format of David O. Watson's book, *Talk With Your Hands*.

The index is in two parts: first comes an alphabetically arranged Basic Word Index of 340 entries; second is a Sign Language Index alphabetically listing the 590 signs described in the manual.

Because this is not *per se* a lesson plan or course of study outline, the success of the manual would depend on the teacher and the practice materials he might devise to teach his classes.

*4. Bornstein, Harry, Lillian Hamilton, Barbara Kannapell, Howard Roy, and Karen Saulnier. *Basic Pre-School Signed-English Dictionary.* Washington, D.C.: Gallaudet College Press, 1973.

This dictionary, containing about 1100 signs, is one part of a system used to teach Signed English. It uses two kinds of gestures, signed words and markers (i.e. -s, -ing, -ed). This system is being developed by the joint effort of the Gallaudet Psychology Department and the Gallaudet Pre-School. It is partially supported by a grant from the U.S. Office of Education.

The Gallaudet Pre-School Signed English Project system is designed to assist in English language development of pre-school children through the use of various, coordinated teaching materials. The materials include the aforementioned dictionary, story books, songs and posters, all in Signed English. A vocabulary list of about 2500 words used by young children is the basic content.

The materials are designed to be read aloud and the signs and markers used as a manual aid to learning English. The materials will be graded from 18 months to 5 years for continued use by pre-schoolers.

At this time (August 1973) the following list of materials in Signed English has been or is soon to be published: Basic Pre-School Signed-English Dictionary; Storybooks: Little Red Riding Hood, Goldilocks and the Three Bears, Nursery Rhymes from Mother Goose, Hansel and Gretel, The Three Little Pigs, Tommy's Day, Mealtime at the Zoo, Songs, Songs with a record; Posters: Rock-a-bye Baby and Jack and Jill. At press: I Want to be a Farmer, The Night Before Christmas, The Three Little Kittens and Spring is Green.

Additional material will be published in the future as the program expands, including more storybooks and an expansion of the dictionary. Further information can be obtained from Dr. Bornstein's office at Gallaudet in the Psychology Department.

5. Bornstein, Harry, Lillian Hamilton and Barbara Kannapell. *Signs for Instructional Purposes.* Washington, D.C.: Gallaudet College Press, 1969.

As the title indicates, this book contains signs developed specifically for instructional purposes. Development of these signs was undertaken by the Office of Institutional Research and members of the faculty at Gallaudet College in an attempt to represent, with individual signs, those usually lengthy words and phrases which, because they are important to a subject matter, are frequently used in class.

This book, *Signs for Instructional Purposes,* the outcome of their efforts, is a dictionary of 465 signs which have been classified according to four educational divisions: (1) Science and Mathematics, (2) Humanities, (3) Social Studies, (4) Professional Studies. Each division has a section devoted to words common to all subjects in that division, as well as sections for terms in specific subject areas.

Those already proficient with the language of signs can most readily appreciate the five basic rationales used for sign invention: (1) an existing sign with a letter cue, (2) a compound of two existing signs, (3) a compound of a letter and an existing sign, (4) a completely new sign, and (5) a new sign with a letter cue. In addition, consultants created a small number of signs "spontaneously," i.e., without any construction guide. The supplementary notations printed with the illustrations indicate placement, movement and configuration of the hands, as well as the existing sign, if any, used in making the new sign.

The illustrations by Betty Miller are sufficiently descriptive and clear that those familiar with sign language should be able to reproduce the signs without further help. The only difficulty with Miss Miller's illustrations is this: "reading" illustrated signs and reproducing them accurately become more difficult when there is no body orientation to rely on. The work done by Stokoe underscored the fact that there are three necessary elements in any sign: the *dez* (configuration of the hands), the *sig* (the movement) and the *tab* (the part of the body in which the sign is made). While eliminating the body outline makes the illustrations crisp and uncluttered (there is no "noise"), it also eliminates the background locus that is the basis for *tab* elements in signing.

Reproduced in black on a white background, with red lines and arrows to indicate the appropriate motions, five to six illustrations appear on each page. The text is small (5½″ x 9″); but, the balance and variety of the page layouts and the inherent attractiveness of the illustrations themselves, enhance the text and make study of the dictionary a pleasant experience.

One other notable feature is the use of both the English and French languages in the printed text. So that a larger audience might find the text useful, each sign is labeled with its French equivalent. All prose discussions are printed in both languages, and a bilingual index is also included.

Recommended especially for those involved in instruction of deaf persons on the secondary and college levels, this book should be studied by all proficient with the language of signs.

One note of caution to readers: because these signs were developed specifically for classroom use, they, at this time, are known to and fill the needs of a numerically small segment of the deaf population.

6. Casterline, Dorothy C., Carl C. Croneberg, and William C. Stokoe, Jr. *A Dictionary of American Sign Language on Linguistic Principles.* Washington, D.C.: Gallaudet College Press, 1965.

The dictionary lists approximately 3000 signs (morphemes) of the American Sign Language in symbolic notation and is as complete an inventory of the lexicon of the language as the state of linguistic analysis will allow. An entry for each sign gives information about its formation, its grammatical and syntactical features—illustrated by brief sign language phrases—an indication of its usage, whether standard, dialectal, formal, or other, and some of its approximate English equivalents. Introductory material explains, with photographic illustrations, the basic structure of signs and the system of symbols used for writing them in an essay on the language and its grammar.

*7. Cokely, Dennis R. and Rev. Rudolph Gawlik. *Options: A Position Paper on the Relationship Between Manual English and Sign.* Washington, D.C.: Kendall Demonstration Elementary School for the Deaf, 1973.

This paper does not attempt to teach signs. Instead, it is a critical review of three Manual English systems and their relationship to Signs. The three systems reviewed are: *Seeing Essential English* (S.E.E. I), David Anthony; *Signing Exact English* (S.E.E. II), Gerilee Gustason; and *Linguistics of Visual English* (L.O.V.E.), Dennis Wampler.

The authors try to avoid focusing on pure vocabulary differences, interesting as they are, and concentrate on the principles of the three Manual English systems and how they relate to one another and to Ameslan (American Sign Language).

The format is simple, the basic principles of LOVE are stated and then cross-references to the two SEE's. Following this comparison of principles are the authors' critical comments and observations for each principle. The principle comparisons make up the bulk of the text. A summary follows.

In the summary, the authors state that "there is no significant difference in the basic principles." Reference is also made, in a positive manner, to these attempts to advance in working with the problems of deaf children in learning the English language.

Finally, the authors give some suggestions and alternate approaches to problems they encountered in the relationship between Manual English and Signs.

8. Davis, Anne. *The Language of Signs: A Handbook for Manual Communication with the Deaf.* New York: Executive Council of the Episcopal Church, 1966.

This handbook contains approximately six hundred and fifty signs which are considered a basic vocabulary for manual communication with deaf persons. The book presents the signs in photograph form, very few with superimposed arrows to indicate the motion of the sign. Generally, the verbal descriptions accompanying each photograph are considered sufficient for duplication. Starting with the manual alphabet and the basic hand positions, the handbook progresses through sixteen discrete categories including "Family Relationships," "People and Professions," "Pronouns," "Time Words," "Verbs," and "Mental Actions." The Supplementary Sections, A through E, contain Church signs and words commonly used in religious services. Some of these signs are peculiar to the Episcopal deaf community. A standard bibliography and an alphabetical index are included.

The book is complete in itself and the clarity of the photographs will permit its use as an independent study tool for teacher and student. To facilitate its use with the 8mm training films, "The Sign Language of the Deaf," the words are listed as they appear on the films. The sections of the handbook are also numbered to correspond with the reels of film in the series.

9. Falberg, Roger M. *The Language of Silence*. Wichita, Kansas: Deaf and Hard of Hearing Counseling Service, Inc., 1963.

This book, neither an illustrated textbook nor a technical treatise, explores the subtleties of manual communication and is intended to supplement a good dictionary of signs. Attention is called to the nuances of the language of signs of which only the fluent user is aware. Maximum benefits will accrue to the student who is willing to practice with the deaf themselves after learning the manual alphabet and acquiring a basic vocabulary of signs.

The author emphasizes the relation of signs to their referents (picture concepts) and cautions that the language of signs stands somewhere in between picture-language and written language on the development scale. From his point of view, the language of the deaf is more directly traceable to referents than is oral language.

A distinct feature of this book is a lesson plan which provides explanations and practice within troublesome areas, such as the formation of the tenses; the use of function words, the negatives, the possessives, the compulsion words (must, demand-require, need, furnish-possess-must), the comparatives, and time indicators; the refinements to have, has, and had; words with multiple referents; and the highly developed use of flowing signs in poetry and songs.

Falberg also attempts a broad classification of the more commonly used signs: (1) signs that show structure, (2) signs that show function, and (3) the spatial indicators, i.e., pointing or showing the position of referents in real space.

An appendix contains pointers in the use of the manual alphabet, an exercise in the formation of numbers, and a vocabulary checklist which refers one to descriptions of signs and their nuances as discussed in the text.

Spiral binding makes it possible for the reader to open the book flat, leaving both hands free for practice. There are, however, only a few illustrations and descriptions of signs —used to clarify certain applications.

*10. Fant, Louie J. *Ameslan: An Introduction to American Sign Language*. Silver Spring, Maryland: National Association of the Deaf, 1972.

Presented through a well designed combination of photographs and written explanations, this text attempts to teach Ameslan (American Sign Language), as deaf people use and combine signs. The rules of Ameslan are presented and contrasted, at times, with those of English. Explanations of Ameslan and Siglish are also provided in the introduction.

Approximately 375 signs are covered in the text, which is neither a dictionary nor a self-teaching device. The signs and their combination are taught through the use of poetry, conversation, dialogues and monologues. The text is a concise, effective, and unique approach to teaching Sign language.

Also designed for use with the book are 14 movies containing the text items taught. The films can be used with the text, where indicated, for the purpose of review and practice of receptive abilities.

In the Appendix are two additional sections. One section is an outline on how to indicate time relationships, the other is on question form indications.

A teacher's guide is also available as described in the next entry.

*11. Fant, Louie J. *Ameslan: An Introduction to American Sign Language–Teacher's Guide*. Silver Spring, Maryland, National Association of the Deaf, 1972.

This 12-page teacher's guide contains suggestions as to text usage, materials and media that may be used, specific comments about problems, and important points to remember while teaching.

The pamphlet corresponds to the text's lessons and numbered sections to provide easy access and usage.

The guide is only available with orders of ten or more books or with a film package.

12. Fant, Louie J. *Say It With Hands*. Washington, D.C.: *American Annals of the Deaf*, Gallaudet College, 1964.

This book offers a good lesson plan to be used by any teacher of the language of signs. It is also a good reference book for those who have already had a course in the language of signs and for students to use providing they have an opportunity to practice with someone who is proficient in receptive and expressive languages of signs. It should be emphasized that the author intended this book as a lesson plan rather than a dictionary.

There is some well-written introductory material on the nature of the language of signs, hints on learning fingerspelling, the importance of facial expression and body movements, and an explanation of the lesson plan. This introduction gives the beginning student an explanation and understanding of the basic aspects of the language of signs.

The 46 lessons and the grouping of signs are built around handshapes, because the author believes that one will learn the signs more readily and remember them more easily by this method. All signs made while the hands are in the A shape constitute one lesson, those made with closed fists another, and so on. This book contains valuable tips on shortcuts, abbreviations, and sign language etiquette. At the end of each lesson are practice sentences which not only contain material learned in that lesson, but also many signs learned in previous lessons. These sentences also provide fingerspelling practice. The drawings showing the execution of signs are adequate for the intended use of the book.

13. Guillory, LaVera M. *Expressive and Receptive Fingerspelling for Hearing Adults*. Baton Rouge, Louisiana: Claitor's Book Store, 1966.

This manual is an attempt to present a pedagogically consistent method for teaching fingerspelling to adult hearing persons with fully developed reading and writing skills.

The author points out that a resurgence of interest in fingerspelling was caused by the introduction of the Rochester Method of Instruction to the School for the Deaf in Baton Rouge, Louisiana. Recognizing that fingerspelling requires receptive as well as expressive skills, and that the speed of the practitioner precludes the reading of individual letters, the author hypothesized that fingerspelling might be taught through application of the *phonetic method* of teaching reading and writing. (Readers should note that phonetic symbols cannot be duplicated manually, and thus, the designation "phonetic method of fingerspelling" is a misnomer. However, since no apt alternative designation has suggested itself, the term "phonetic method" will be used throughout this review.) This manual is a plan for learning to fingerspell the basic phonetic elements found in the English language instead of learning the individual letters of the manual alphabet.

In the introductory material the author stresses that the student must see *whole words* in receiving the fingerspelled message and he must spell and speak *whole words simultaneously* when expressing the fingerspelled messages. Common faults in fingerspelling and hints for expressive and receptive fingerspelling are included in this section along with "The First Lesson and Introduction to Phonetic Fingerspelling" which is a demonstration of the syllabication recommended for clear fingerspelling with simultaneous speech.

There are 23 pages of drill material in this manual. Beginning with two-letter configurations, the author drills each phonetic element by adding initial letters to make an English word until the whole family of words has been mastered. For example, the basic phonetic element *ab* is drilled as cab, dab, gab and so on.

Forty-seven basic phonetic units are drilled in this manner, the accompanying illustrations in black line drawings introducing the proper hand configurations. Beginning with the phonetic units starting with the letter "a," the drills proceed through the e-, i-, o- and u- phonetic units. The letters of the manual alphabet are not taught individually and the illustrations of the alphabet are appended solely for purposes of reference and clarity.

Variety is introduced with the nonsense sentences composed of three-letter rhyme words, followed by four-letter word drills and practice sentences using both the three- and four-letter words.

Commonly used words, conversational sentences, selected long words, digraphs (two-letter combinations representing one sound) and digraph words, prefixes and suffixes are drilled in separate lessons. The syllabication drill focuses on compounds and words formed with prefixes and suffixes.

This manual is best-suited for classroom situations where a teacher can observe the drill practice of groups of students and recommended individual practice "therapy" where necessary.

*14. Gustason, Gerilee, Donna Pfetzing, and Ester Zawolkow. *Signing Exact English: Seeing Instead of Hearing.* Rossmoor, California: Modern Sign Press, 1972.

This manual, basically a dictionary, takes a recent approach to the use of signs. It uses signs (not Sign Language) to present, in visual form, the words and affixes of a standard set of vocabulary items in English.

Included in the manual are approximately 1700 signs, each with its own line drawing, explanations where necessary, depicting each of 1700 different words or affixes. About 90 of the signs are listed in three categories, Be Verbs and Modals, Pronouns, and Affixes, while the remaining 1600 are listed alphabetically in a vocabulary section.

The introduction sets forth most of the principles and rationale for the use of signs to teach and expand English. The manual can be a good foundation to aid language deficient students.

Also contained within the manual are line drawings of the hand positions in the Manual Alphabet and the numbers from one to ten. The Pledge of Allegiance as an example of Exact English usage also appears.

15. Hoemann, Harry W., Ed. *Improved Techniques of Communication: A Training Manual for Use with Severely Handicapped Deaf Clients.* Bowling Green State University, 1970.

The difficulties faced by rehabilitation workers with the language handicapped deaf adult in Lapeer and Lansing, Michigan in teaching the basic English skills necessary for a prelingually deaf adult to function in the world of work are familiar to all involved with deaf education. For these particular workers in Michigan, however, concern with the problem took concrete form in a workshop of deaf professionals sponsored by Catholic University in Knoxville, Tennessee, in August, 1967. The Michigan rehabilitation workers had found that manual communication is a valid instructional medium; however, because the manual communication system and the system of written English are different, conventional sign language could not be used to reinforce the patterns of English. By developing signs that would bring the manual communication system into a visible English form for classroom use, and extracurricular conversation, perhaps reinforcement of basic English Language patterns would ensue.

This manual, the outcome of the workshop, has as its outstanding feature "A Prescriptive Dictionary for Improved Manual Communication," which aims to reduce the discrepancies between the conventional sign language of the deaf and the English language. This illustrated dictionary, appearing on pages 6-52, does not aim at standardization of signs; it is an approach to the problem, rather than a fixed symbol system.

Individual signs for prefixes (e.g., re-, pre-), suffixes (e.g., -tion, -ment), inflected forms of auxiliary verbs (have, has, had), forms of the verb *to be* (am, are, was, were), indicators for past and participial forms (-ed, -ing), pronouns, selected prepositions and conjunctions, were developed to reduce syntactical discrepancies. Reduction of lexical discrepancies was encouraged by the development of signs for such categories as measurements, work-oriented words, money matters, vehicles, wearing apparel. Signs defying such classification are grouped as: selected adjectives and adverbs, initialized verbs and nouns (i.e., signs made with a lead-letter), and ideographic nouns (i.e., signs whose forms resemble the referent).

Developed for rehabilitation workers with the adult deaf who are proficient in sign language and who are attempting to improve the English language skills of deaf clients, the manual contains 261 numbered entries. Not all of these entries are illustrated, the editor presupposing that proficiency with manual communication would enable the user to reproduce the sign from the verbal notations that sometimes appear *in lieu* of illustrations.

The task remains for the rehabilitation worker to devise lessons to teach the basic English language concepts and to teach the signs which make visible and reinforce those concepts, thus encouraging simultaneous development of the sign language vocabulary and English language vocabulary in the language handicapped deaf adult.

Those concerned with the teaching of language to the deaf may profit from a study of this dictionary and the accompanying discussions, "Increasing Compatibility between Sign Language and English," and "Techniques for Using Improved Manual Communication as a Language Training Tool."

16. Kosche, Martin. *Hymns for Signing and Singing.* (Write to author, 116 Walnut Street, Delavan, Wisconsin 53115.)

Rev. Kosche has developed a book of hymns suitable for rendering in the language of signs by copying many of the songs in the *Lutheran Hymnal* and suggesting suitable signs for difficult words. The full line of a hymn as it appears in the original is reproduced, and suggested sign substitutions appear over the original words. In this manner, the same book can be used by normal hearing people during Lutheran church services. The author acknowledges that the book is still in rough form, and invites suggestions for improvement. There are occasional footnotes containing descriptions of how to make signs that are not too well-known, such as "veins" and "throne."

While the book is best suited for use by someone already familiar with the language of signs, beginning interpreters might obtain some clues from the substitutions suggested for words often used during religious services.

17. Landes, Robert M. *Approaches: A Digest of Methods in Learning the Language of Signs.* Richmond, Virginia: 1968. (Write to Virginia Baptist General Board, P.O. Box 8568, Richmond, Virginia 23226.)

This manual, *Approaches*, purports to be a "Digest of Methods in Learning the Language of Signs." However, because this manual never considers extant methods for learning this language, it cannot present a condensation of those methods, nor a considered discussion of them. One wishes that the primary difficulty here were generated solely by the misleading character of the title.

The essential problem is in pedagogy. The author's approach is eclectic. Be assured that eclecticism does not necessarily generate disorder; and, in many teaching situations, an eclectic approach is commendable. The criticism is this: because the manual has no inherently unified program for developing graded skills, it fails to offer a coherent pedagogical basis for teaching or learning.

This course, designed to teach a basic sign language, requires three additional texts: a dictionary of signs, a publication of the Department of Health, Education, and Welfare, called "Orientation of Social Workers to the Problems of Deaf Persons," and George B. Joslin's manual for the Southern Baptist Convention, "Manual for Work With the Deaf."

In Chapter 2, "Fingerspelling and the Manual Alphabet," the author presents some mnemonic aids that are of note, and which will be useful to students who have difficulty remembering the configuration of individual letters of the manual alphabet. Chapters 3 through 5 introduce specific factors for consideration by students of sign language and interpretation, but the discussions are marred by imprecise definition and categorization.

One of the cardinal rules of sign language is "sign what you mean, not what you say." Landes exemplifies this concisely and well in Chapter 3 when he lists 31 sentences using the word *run* and indicates the different concept conveyed in each sentence.

Practice materials are introduced with the explanation of the number system in Chapter 7. This is a thorough description of the counting procedure and also describes the method for denoting scriptural chapter and verse numbers in sign language.

The remaining chapters, 8-26, constitute the bulk of the text and are consistent in format, the vocabulary study followed by practical sentences and a lesson from *The Story of Jesus* by Frank C. Laubach. The author asserts that the aim of the textbook is "to teach a basic sign language, and to that end the materials should be followed as closely as possible in order to assure continuity and progression of thought." The text format itself presents numerous problems: the stories from the *Life of Christ* are included for the purpose of developing interpreting insights and two per class should be read. A class of students learning sign language will neither have the vocabulary nor the skill to interpret these stories. Further, the basic vocabulary study for each chapter is not consistently reinforced by the practical sentences nor the stories.

By collating the stories in an appendix with appropriate vocabulary practice (the names of Biblical persons and places), students will be saved the necessity of thumbing through material for which they are not yet ready.

Only if the teacher presents a carefully prepared basic introduction to the language of signs, using a good dictionary, will this text be of any use. The teacher will remain the informant for the class and will produce the drill materials in fingerspelling and the language of signs necessary to establish basic competency.

The manual might in fact be more successful if it were aimed at persons who have completed a basic course in the language of signs and are now able to undertake a new course with a specialized focus, the text being specifically designed for use by religious groups who have ministries to the deaf.

The second edition of *Approaches*, published in 1969, is, according to the preface, "revised only slightly and then only in order to clarify meaning." In fact, the revision excises only a few sentences and does not focus on the essential difficulties in the text. The criticisms for the first text remain applicable to the second edition.

The now-printed text, compiled in a 7" x 10" three-ring loose-leaf binder, permits the pages of the text to lie flat. The pagination has been changed to simple numerical order, and this is a decided improvement over the chapter-page system of the original. Some of the illustrations have been changed. These simple improvements make the text visually more pleasing.

Chapter 27, "Resources," has been retained unchanged in the second edition.

18. Long, J. Schuyler. *The Sign Language: A Manual of Signs*. Washington, D.C.: Gallaudet College, 1962. Reprint of second edition.

Dr. Long stated that the purpose of his book was to provide a standard reference for those desiring to learn the language of signs, for those desiring to refresh their memories, and for those desiring to learn unfamiliar signs.

Further, he stated that he wishes to fulfill what he felt was a need of deaf persons for a standard by which the usage of the original, pure, and accurate signs would be perpetuated.

The book contains over 1400 signs, all of which have written descriptions and photographs showing the position for making the signs. Arrows are used to illustrate the movements involved in executing each of the manual symbols. The signs are grouped under chapter headings such as Numbers and Counting, Animals, Auxiliary Verbs, Occupations, etc. There is an alphabetical index of all terms.

There is a chapter on the history, development, and usage of both the language of signs and fingerspelling. Also included is a brief, but clear explanation of the role of manual communication in the social and educational life of deaf people. The book concludes with pictorial representations of sample sentences, the Lord's Prayer, and an appendix of Catholic signs.

The Sign Language is primarily a dictionary of signs, not a manual of the language of signs. Study of the book without the assistance of a competent instructor will not make for facility in manual communication. It is one of the early references on the language of signs. The original photographs have been retained in the 1963 reprint and are consequently outdated and detract from the appeal of the book.

*19. Madsen, Willard J. *Conversational Sign Language II: An Intermediate-Advanced Manual.* Washington, D.C.: Gallaudet College Press, 1972.

This book is a valuable contribution to the library of printed material available to teachers and students of the language of signs. Unique in its emphasis on continued instruction for those who have completed a basic course in manual communication, the book encourages the development of skills in conversing in the "idiom" of the deaf adult.

Originally a mimeographed manual, the revised version is much improved, both in content and form, and it is greatly expanded.

As with the mimeographed edition, the text is divided into three parts, I–"A Review of Basic Sign Language and Fingerspelling," II–"English Idioms," and III–"Sign Language Idioms." The information is presented in lesson form. Each lesson is limited in content so as to provide for an easy and convenient size. The lessons also have a set of practice sentences for practice. A practice test is provided every three lessons for use as review material.

Part I consists of 30 lessons beginning with fingerspelling and moving through such groupings as time-space relationships, food and drink, cities, money, numbers, and various others. The entire section covers about 750 words with written explanation on how to form the signs. This section has been expanded from the previous 500 words.

Part II contains 15 lessons and covers some 220 English idioms presented with Sign Language translations. The idioms are expanded to some 300 Sign language usages.

Part III has had the largest revision with an increase of some 150 Sign language idioms to a total of about 300. The idioms are grouped, as much as possible, by broken English patterns that approximate the sign equivalents such as "for-for" or "do-do" and are arranged in lessons according to these patterns. Where there are no patterns written descriptions of the signs are given.

Parts I and II are indexed together by English word translation, while Part III is indexed separately by the broken English pattern. Those idioms without patterns are not indexed.

The text is not self-teaching for there are few line drawings for individual signs, also a competent instructor is required to give the appropriate rendition of the Sign language idioms. The publication of this text therefore allows for intermediate and advanced levels of Sign language classes to have their own text.

20. Riekehof, Lottie L. *Talk To the Deaf.* Springfield, Missouri: Gospel Publishing House, 1963. (1445 Booneville Avenue, Springfield, Missouri 65802)

Talk to the Deaf, subtitled "A practical visual guide useful to any one wishing to master the sign language and the manual alphabet," by Lottie Riekehof of the Central Bible Institute of Springfield, Missouri, is a glossary of about 100 basic signs.

The book is divided into three major sections: "A Brief History of the Sign Language," "Learning to Use the Sign Language and the Manual Alphabet," and finally the main portion, "Sign Language." In this book signs are classified into 25 categories. The format for presenting the various signs consists of simple word descriptions accompanied with synonyms and illustrations. Movements are indicated by broken line drawings and arrows. The author stresses the importance of studying the word descriptions in conjunction with the synonyms. Drawings depict the various signs and are supplemented by descriptions.

21. Sanders, Josef I., Ed. *The ABC's of Sign Language.* Tulsa, Oklahoma: Manca Press, Inc., 1968.

According to the preface, this book was designed "to provide a pre-primer, an easy palatable introduction to the language of signs for the uninitiated." And it is precisely this pre-primer approach of *The ABC's of Sign Language* that produces the indelible impression in the reader that the "uninitiated" of the preface are children.

Following the pattern of numerous abecedarian books for children, the editor and illustrator have produced a sturdy, hard-bound picture book dictionary of 126 signs. The format is attractive and consistent; James Harrell's illustrations are realistic and easy to "read."

Each of the 126 signs presented in the book is given two full 8½" x 11" pages. The individual letters of the manual alphabet and the numbers one through twenty, the numbers 100, 500 and 1000 are each given one page in the text. The format for the signs is as follows: the word is centered on the left-hand page in large upper-case letters with verbal directions for making the signs printed immediately below. On the right-hand page are the illustrations for the sign (with arrows indicating the appropriate movements), an illustration of the referent itself and immediately below, the word *re*printed in lower case letters.

The 126 nouns thus illustrated are accurately termed a basic recognition vocabulary (both in the English language and the language of signs) for children. Such entries as "jump rope," "oil well," "wagon" and "zoo" are further indications of this. One difficulty that a young audience might encounter, however, would be reading the verbal descriptions of the signs.

Adults would need neither the referrents pictured, nor the reinforcement provided by the repetition of the printed word. In fact, the "uninitiated" adult would be more inclined to make a present of this book to a child. However, the price, which is itself prohibitive would foster "browsing" instead of buying.

22. Siger, Leonard C. "Gestures, the Language of Signs, and Human Communication," *American Annals of the Deaf*, Vol. 113: 1, pp. 11-28, January, 1968.

In this article, originally delivered as a paper at the Warburg Institute of the University of London on June 19, 1967, Dr. Siger cites various historical instances of the use of gesture systems and manual communication. Having always been a part of human behavior, gesture systems were not specifically devised for purposes of educating deaf persons.

Venerable Bede, an ecclesiastical historian, calls attention to the use of manual counting systems as early as the 8th century. For purposes of illustration, Dr. Siger has included photographic copies of two 10th century manuscripts that depict manual counting systems. Not until 1600, with the publication of Bonet's *Reducción de las latras* in Spain (from which our one-handed manual alphabet is derived), do we get the first full-length work on deaf education.

Previous to this, consistent gesture systems were developed as counting systems, mnemonic aids, or as part of an orator's training and practice. Ancient rhetoricians, taking Quintillian as a favored guide, were practiced in the art of gesture. During the Renaissance, the art of gesture in Rhetoric was revived, such orators as John Donne being noted for matching the elegance of delivery to the elegance of words.

Gestures are also captured in the Renaissance paintings of the late 15th century through 17th century. As examples, Dr. Siger presents five figures depicting the use of rhetorical gestures in painting. Chosen from the works of Luini, Pinturicchio, Campi and Durer, each painting is a representation of the New Testament theme of the "Dispute in the Temple."

A discussion, with accompanying photographs, of the Symbolic Gestures of the Japanese Buddhists is also included.

Then, Dr. Siger undertakes a discussion of the history of the language of sings of the American Deaf, from its beginning at the French institute of Abbé de l'Épée, to its introduction into the United States by Thomas Hopkins Gallaudet, to its use today. Special note is made of its existence in the National Theater of the Deaf, where, beyond stating the facts of a case or telling the news as in ordinary conversation, it carries, as Dr. Siger says, "the challenging burden of poetic statement."

Dr. Siger's paper is of value to all who are interested in the historical foundations and vestiges of gesture systems in human communication. The paper is itself a fine example of a brief, scholarly, carefully documented research work.

23. Springer, C. J. *Talking With the Deaf*. Baton Rouge, Louisiana: Redemptorist Fathers, 1961. (5354 Plank Road, Baton Rouge, Louisiana 70805)

This is an illustrated dictionary of the language of signs containing approximately 1000 terms. Each sign is briefly described verbally and clearly presented pictorially by one or two photographs, some of which have arrows indicating the movements involved in the execution of the sign.

The terminology presented in this text covers basic vocabulary with some emphasis on religious signs. The manual alphabet is presented, but discussion of numbers and counting is limited to digits one through twelve. The signs are presented in alphabetical order, in contrast to most of this type, which group them by subject or by parts of speech. However, a valuable cross-index of signs that have more than one meaning in English is included.

It is felt that this book would be a suitable text in a course on the language of signs, though it is less complete in the number and scope of its terms than are some other available books. The text would be of particular value for a person interested in religious interpreting for Catholic Church work and even work with other denominations, as the religious signs given can be used "regardless of religious affiliation" according to the author.

It is noted that this book is often confused with Father Higgins' text, "How to Talk to the Deaf." Actually, it is an updating of this earlier work and a much more appropriate book for today's student of the language of signs.

24. Stokoe, William C., Jr. *Sign Language Structure: An Outline of the Visual Communication Systems of the American Deaf*. Buffalo, New York: University of Buffalo, 1960. (Studies in Linguistics, Occasional Papers 8)

The monograph by Stokoe represents a different approach to the study and teaching of the language of signs. Stokoe has applied the principles of structural linguistics to the visual communication system of the language of signs. He has attempted to identify the minimal distinctive units of this language which correspond to the phonemes of spoken language.

For the purpose of this review, only the application of Stokoe's system to the teaching of the language of signs will be discussed. Stokoe has identified the minimal distinctive features of this language and classified them into three groups. These groups are: "tab," "dez," and "sig." A knowledge of the symbols within these groups will enable the beginning student of the language of signs to produce any sign.

The symbols grouped under the title of "tab" refer to the part of the body in which the sign is made, for example, at the forehead or the chest. Those symbols under "dez" refer to the configuration of the hands in making the sign. The symbols under the "sig" classification indicate the movement which should be made to produce the correct sign. A knowledge of the symbols in these three classifications—"tab," "dez," and "sig"—will enable the student of the language of signs to understand the area of the body in which the sign should be made, the configuration of the hands in making the signs, and the motion of the hands necessary to produce the sign.

*25. Stokoe, William C. *The Study of Sign Language*. Silver Spring, Maryland: National Association of the Deaf, revised 1971.

An analysis of Sign language, this study looks at Sign language and its relationship to English and Education of the Deaf. Five areas involving Sign language are considered: how language may be presented to the eye; the composition of Sign language; bilingualism and Sign language; social implications of Sign language; and concerns for teachers in use and practical classroom research of Sign language.

Originally commissioned by the ERIC Clearinghouse for Linguistics, this study is a linguistic analysis and technical look at Sign language written for those with some linguistic background.

The revised 1971 version is presently out of print, however, the original edition on microfiche or in hard copy by writing to the Eric Document Reproduction Service, 4827 Rugby Avenue, Bethesda, Maryland 20014.

*26. Washington State School for the Deaf, The. *An Introduction to Manual English*. Vancouver, Washington: The Washington State School for the Deaf, 1972.

This text for learning Manual English is basically a dictionary to be used in class with a competent instructor. The book employs line drawings for some 1000 word/sign equivalents used in Manual English. The word/signs are grouped according to English grammar classifications, Affixes and Contractions, Pronouns, Verbs, Adjectives, etc. A fingerspelling alphabet and extensive number chart are also included in illustrated form.

The front matter contains a large amount of information on usage of the text. Included in this information are explanations on specific fingerspelling techniques and problems, how to make number handshapes, an extensive write-up on how to read the line drawings, and suggestions on use and when to learn the affixes.

Also included in the front matter is an article on Rationale for Manual English (and Total Communication) as it is used at the Washington State School.

The final portion of the front matter is a set of line drawings entitled, "How to 'Put it all Together'," in which sentences with line drawings for the signs show how to combine the signs, fingerspelling and affixes together in proper English syntax and grammar to form Manual English.

27. Watson, David O. *Talk With Your Hands*. Menasha, Wisconsin: George Banta Company, 1963. (Write to author, Route 1, Winneconne, Wisconsin 54986.)

A lively, conversational style of approach is used by David O. Watson, author and illustrator of *Talk With Your Hands*, a book on the American language of signs. The attractiveness of the format and the uniqueness of approach brought instant popularity to the book when it first appeared in 1964. Words, phrases, expressions, and sentences are cleverly executed in the language of signs with life-like illustrations of hand positioning that are supplemented by engaging comic-page figures that lend a realistic touch to the total presentation.

The dynamic appeal of Mr. Watson's illustrations is further heightened by the use of red lines and arrows to indicate the direction the hands are to take in forming a sign. The flash of red over black on an otherwise all-white background relieves the tediousness that often goes with deciphering directions. The many body positions that are used throughout the book also relieve tedium and give a warm human quality to the language of signs.

Mr. Watson offers sign symbols for approximately 1700 words and terms. He has grouped them mainly under subject headings. All those parts of speech that are ordinarily needed for satisfactory presentation of a subject are included. These words are not identified as parts of speech. This is in keeping with the disregard the language of signs has for the grammatical rules that govern the use of spoken and written language. Mr. Watson does, however, show how the language of signs can be used syntactically. He does this by inserting fingerspelled words where they are needed to form grammatically correct sentences.

In a number of instances, the index refers the reader to more than one page number. This is because of the multiple meanings of many words which are carried over into the language of signs in the form of multiple sign symbols. This particular feature of the book should be a great help to readers who are unaware of the opportunity and need for being selective in use of signs.

*28. Watson, David O. *Talk With Your Hands, Volumes I and II*. Menasha, Wisconsin: George Banta Company, 1973.

This new updated version of Mr. Watson's dictionary has been expanded by 450-500 new signs into two volumes. Emphasis is placed on aiding small deaf children learn signs and the use of deaf idioms of Ameslan by hearing persons.

The format presents vocabulary material in subject groupings in Volume I. Volume II contains additional signs in both subject groupings and hand position groupings, practice sentences and general signs.

New categories of signs are "Away from Home," "Signs Used in and Around the House," and "Things Kids Like to Talk About."

1. Abelson, Bambii Rae. *Alpha-Hands Flash Cards.* Buffalo, New York: Kenworthy Educational Service, Inc., 1969.

This teaching aid contains fifty-two 5½″ x 8½″ illustrated flash cards with letters of the manual alphabet, days of the week, numbers one through ten, names of colors (5), close family relative classifications (uncle, aunt, cousin), and a parent-teacher manual.

Mrs. Abelson states in her manual that the

> ALPHA-HANDS FLASH CARDS have been created for the purpose of providing a realistic method in *communication between* the HEARING and the DEAF. A primary function of this teaching device is to aid parents in INTRODUCING LANGUAGE to a deaf child years BEFORE he may enter school.

She goes on to discuss such topics as "Language," "How the Hearing Can Use the Alpha-Hands Flash Cards," "How to Teach Language to the Deaf Child," "How Does a Deaf Child Learn to Differentiate His Feelings." No topic is discussed with the necessary depth, and the brevity and superficiality of each discussion precludes the development of a philosophy and method of language teaching. Without this, the flash cards will remain useless for concerned parents of young deaf children. The section "How to Shape a Letter" will be sufficient to demonstrate the basic problem. The directions appear as follows:

> View an Alpha-Hands Flash Card and with your RIGHT HAND about 6″ in front of your body imitate the hand position. Try forming two or three letters in this manner. Often it is helpful to do this in front of a mirror. Repeat this procedure daily using 2 or 3 different letters. Practice until you don't have to think letters but they automatically fall from your hand. Within two weeks you will know the entire Manual Alphabet . . .

A cursory inspection of the flash cards indicates discrepancies in the author's understanding of and familiarity with the manual alphabet and the basic signs included in the set. The manual alphabet is perceived differently by the signer and by the receiver. However, this fact is ignored in both the flash cards and the accompanying manual. The cards for the letters "a," "q" and "r," the numbers one through ten, "Sunday" and "Thursday" appear as they would to the person reproducing them.

The remaining letters and signs appear as they would to the person receiving the finger-spelled or signed message. The author has either forgotten to specify this, or she is unaware of the fact.

The cards for "red" and "orange" do not take into account the necessity for body orientation. The same difficulty occurs with "uncle," "aunt" and "cousin" and, further, the movements indicated for these signs are also incorrect. Persons familiar with the language of signs would be unable to "read" these signs.

Also included is the "v," recognized by a majority of Americans as symbolic of the peace movement. However, it is *not* the sign for peace of the American Sign Language of the Deaf.

The flash cards are illustrated on both sides. One side pictures the hand configuration with the letter or word printed above it. On the reverse side, only the hand configuration is shown. Since no explanation is included, one would assume that the parent or teacher, after becoming proficient with fingerspelling, might use the cards to quiz the child's recognition of letters and numbers.

2. Babbini, Barbara E. (Writer and technical advisor) *American Manual Alphabet.* (8mm cartridge) Training Films Series (Graphic Film Corporation Series), Media Services and Captioned Films, BEH/USOE.

The "American Manual Alphabet" is a training film series produced by Graphic Film Corporation for the U.S. Office of Education, Captioned Films for the Deaf. The series comprises 25 lessons and 5 tests, and is available on cartridges for use with the silent standard 8mm Technicolor Projector, Models 200, 200Z, 200WA, 500, 500Z, 500WA, 500WS, 600, 600AD, 700A, 800, 800WA, and 800WS.

The first grouping of four units introduces the manual alphabet and encourages fluency development. The fifth unit in this grouping is a test.

The second grouping, the largest (6 units) grouping of unit materials, focuses on speed-building and progresses through combinations of letters, double vowels, and consonants. "Accuracy: Do's and Don'ts" is one unit in the group. Numbers are introduced in the last two units.

The remaining 15 practice units have been arbitrarily separated into 4 groups, each followed by a test. Each unit presents a rapid drill of letter groups. For example: Unit 18 drills the combinations BO-BR-BL-CA; Unit 20 drills TH-QU-EX.

Such a film series will be invaluable to teachers of beginning courses in Sign Language.

*3. "Bernard Bragg Series"—Southern Regional Media Center for the Deaf, 1814 Lake Avenue, Knoxville, Tennessee 37916.

This series of tapes includes five programs: "Dramatics with Bernard Bragg;" "An Evening with Bernard Bragg;" "People, You and Me;" "Sign Mime: The Language of Drama;" and "Yesterday, and Tomorrow," and totals 2½ hours of actual running time.

The programs would be of interest to classes in Sign language to demonstrate what can be done with the Language of Signs; and would demonstrate various forms of signing such as sign-mime, dramatic Sign language, and dramatics.

The programs are also of interest to demonstrate the wide range of capabilities of sign language as applied to various dramatic art forms.

The series can be obtained from the Southern Regional Media Center by sending them 2½ hours of blank videotape and the program or series title. For no charge, except return postage, the Center will duplicate the programs and return the tapes. For additional information and a catalogue write to the Southern Regional Media Center for the Deaf.

*4. "Children's Playing Cards"—National Association of the Deaf, 814 Thayer Avenue, Silver Spring, Maryland 20910.

These regulation-size playing cards were developed to aid children and their parents to learn signs. The deck contains 26 simple child's vocabulary words like cow, baby, and cup. There are two cards for each word, totaling 52. Each pair of cards contains one card with a four-color representation of the object, and a line drawing of the sign; the other card contains the line drawing, plus the printed word.

Included in each deck is a set of instructions for games like "Old Maid," "Go Fish," and "Concentration." The cards are available from the National Association of the Deaf.

5. *Episcopal Church Training Films.* (8mm cartridge) Audio-Visual Library, The Episcopal Church Center, 815 Second Avenue, New York, New York 10017.

The Conference of Church Workers Among the Deaf, working in cooperation with the National Council of the Episcopal Church, has produced 40 black and white Magi-Cartridge reels demonstrating the manual alphabet and the signs for 700 words. Each 8mm reel has a running time of 4 minutes. A word is shown once and followed by two depictions of the sign at a pace slow enough to be followed by the student.

Thirty-four of the reels are devoted to basic vocabulary, and six show signs used in church services, as well as signs for denominational names and such words as God, faith, and redemption. One reel illustrates the Lord's Prayer.

The projector used with these cartridges—which require no threading or rewinding—has a "stop-motion" button on top, which when pressed, will hold the frame steady for purposes of study. The cartridges will automatically repeat themselves unless stopped.

A handbook for students, "The Language of Signs," by Anne Davis, an instructor at the Maryland School for the Deaf, has been prepared for use with these films. The signs are presented in the same order in both the reels and the handbook.

Signs used in these films are, for the most part, clear. They have good background and good basic positions. Different people are used to deliver the signs. A wide variety of subject matter is covered. Some of the signs, however, are incorrect and amateurish and do not always flow smoothly. The most distracting feature, one which could have been edited, is the return of both hands to an "at rest" or clasping position approximately "marriage" after most signs.

*6. Fant, Louie J. "Ameslan: An Introduction to American Sign Language—Films" Joyce Motion Picture Company, 8320 Reseda Boulevard, Northridge, California 91324.

This is a series of 14 films available for receptive practice material based on Louie Fant's book, *Ameslan*. These films are each about 5 minutes long, in color, and housed in Super 8mm cartridges. They can be shown on a Kodak Ektagraphic 120 projector.

The movies contain lesson material presented in the text. Individual signers present the content, which is repeated again by the next signer. The films are available, in a variety of packages, from the National Association of the Deaf, 814 Thayer Avenue, Silver Spring, Maryland 20910 or the Joyce Motion Picture Company.

*7. "Films on Deafness and Hearing Loss"—Total Communications Laboratory, Western Maryland College, Westminster, Maryland 21157.

The five films described below are available from Western Maryland College, Total Communications Laboratory. They cover a wide range of subjects related to sign language and deafness; and they are designed for those interested in deafness, families with deaf members, parents, professionals interested in deafness, and sign language classes.

"We Tiptoed Around Whispering"—This film depicts, through documentary and dramatization, what is experienced by a family, especially the parents, during the time from birth until a child is diagnosed as deaf.

Scripted by Joanne Greenberg, author of "In This Sign," this 30-minute, color, 16mm film is available for a $15.00 rental fee, with or without captions.

"Listen"—This is a technical documentary on the effects of hearing loss. Causes, solutions, and psychological effects are all discussed. Various types of hearing problems are demonstrated through the use of a filtered sound track.

This film can be rented for $15.00. It is 16mm, color, and can be obtained with or without captions.

"Total Communication"—Segments of pre-school classes of deaf children and interviews with parents give some information on total communication. The rationale for total communication is presented in narrative form by Dr. David Denton.

The rental for this 16mm, color, 15-minute film is $8.00 with or without captions.

"Swan Lake: Conversations with Deaf Teenagers"—A compilation of interviews with deaf teenagers at the Junior National Association of the Deaf Camp, Penguilly, Minnesota, the film covers their opinions and feelings on topics as varied as their families, future plans, and views on racial matters.

The film is presented in Sign language with a spoken interpretation as narration. It is available for a $6.00 rental fee. The film is 15 minutes long, 16mm, and in color.

"Intolerable"—Silent, slapstick comedy techniques are used in this experiment to teach basic vocabulary to deaf children. The film is entertaining as well as educational. It is available in 16mm, black and white, for $4.00. The film is 10 minutes long.

8. *Fingerspelling Films.* (8mm cartridge) (The International Communications Foundation Series), Media Services and Captioned Films, BEH/USOE.

Fingerspelling Films is an instructional film series intended for the beginning student in fingerspelling. The series is presented in two sets: Set A: Fingerspelling for Dormitory Counselors, and Set B: Fingerspelling for Rehabilitation Counselors. Each set consists of six cartridges that contain 4½ minutes of silent, color films.

The series is presented on 8mm cartridge, a type of film that is readily useable with a Technicolor 800 Instant Movie Projector. The ease with which the films can be shown, and the general excellence of the film presentation itself, combine to make *Fingerspelling Films* an important contribution to the training material that is available for instruction in basic skills in fingerspelling.

The instructional pattern that is used in both sets is a step-by-step procedure that leads the student through a sequence of experiences of increasing complexity. Instruction in the manual alphabet is offered first, followed by basic words and conversational type of sentences.

Outstanding features of the films are: (1) excellent photography, (2) clarity and naturalness of fingerspelling, (3) two exposures of certain fingerspelled single letters with the second exposure being different from the first; this tends to reinforce learning, (4) skillful use of facial expression to show how it can add meaning to fingerspelled sentences, and (5) gradual increase of speed of delivery.

*9. Hoemann, Harry W. and Shirley A. Hoemann. "Sign Flash Cards." Silver Spring, Maryland: National Association of the Deaf, 1973.

This deck of 500, 2½" x 3½" flash cards, containing about 1200 signs, was developed by Dr. Hoemann and his wife as a supplement and stimulus for mastering Sign language vocabulary in classes.

Each card contains a single, clear line drawing of a sign. On the reverse side is a written explanation on forming the sign. Also included in the written portion of the card is a description of meaning or definition of the sign, an English equivalent, and often, variations in movement or positioning which produce a different sign and English word equivalent, are presented.

Excellent for practice and review of Sign language, the cards are not meant to teach signs to a novice. The cards are available from the National Association of the Deaf.

10. *Pre-Cana Counseling Film.* (16mm) Media Services and Captioned Films, BEH/USOE.

This film deals with premarriage counseling for Catholic persons. It is in the language of signs and fingerspelling and explains the concepts of the Catholic Church about marriage and its religious significance. This is done at a level that could be understood by most deaf young people.

The main use of this film would be to prepare Catholic couples for marriage and to train seminarians in the signs and modes of expression needed for pre-cana counseling. The performers are priests who have a fair competency in the language of signs, but are not fluent.

11. *Say It with Hands*, Louie Fant, Gallaudet College, Washington, D.C. 20002. (Not available)

This is a series of 46 reels based on the lesson plan in Mr. Fant's book, *Say It with Hands*. Color film is used throughout. It is an experimental series and is not for sale. No copies are available.

The use of color in training films seems to be preferable to black-and-white. At times, both side and front views of a fingerspelled letter were used, but this technique does not seem to have been used for the signs, and it might have been helpful. More than one signer was used, and the utilization of deaf persons as signers was especially noted.

Both literal translations and idiomatic sign language expressions were used. Perhaps the transition from one to the other could be made more gradual, however. The question mark was omitted at the end of interrogative forms. The sign made with both hands forming zeros was used alone for "no-one." Usually, a second sign is used in this case, as the double-zero sign alone is most often interpreted as "none."

Technical flaws were evident; however, this is understandable in a low-budget experimental film.

*12. "Say It with Hands Series"—Southern Regional Media Center for the Deaf, 1814 Lake Avenue, Knoxville, Tennessee 37916.

This series of 26, ½-hour television programs provides instruction in manual communication. Based on Fant's book, the series was originally produced by KERA-TV 13 Dallas, and the Callier Hearing and Speech Center of Dallas in cooperation with the NAD Communicative Skills Program and under a contract with Media Services and Captioned Films, Bureau of Education for the Handicapped, Office of Education.

Tapes are available from the Southern Regional Media Center for the Deaf at no charge, except return shipping. To obtain this series send enough blank videotape (13 hours) to cover program time and specify the series title. The Center will duplicate the programs and return them to you. For more information contact the Southern Regional Media Center for the Deaf.

Kinescopes in 16mm are also available through regular Media Services and Captioned Films distribution libraries. Should you wish these films, but do not now have an account with Media Services and Captioned Films, you should write to Dr. Howard Quigley, Director, Educational Materials Distribution Center, 5034 Wisconsin Avenue, N.W., Washington, D.C. 20016.

13. *Sign Language, The.* Media Services and Captioned Films, BEH/USOE.

A story about Thomas H. Gallaudet and a basic vocabulary drill are presented in this experimental film. The language of signs and fingerspelling is used throughout. The section on Gallaudet's life would be useable as a test or practice lesson for advanced students in manual communication. The vocabulary part gives some basic signs and their English equivalents. This film is clearly experimental and introduces some interesting techniques, but is not a technically polished production.

14. *Teaching the Manual Alphabet.* (8mm) Dr. Harry Bornstein, Office of Institutional Research, Gallaudet College, Washington, D.C. 20002.

This is a series of 17 filmed lessons in fingerspelling including two tests. The films are in color and require a variable-speed 8mm projector and a knowledge of how to operate it. The first two lessons introduce the manual alphabet, with individual letters presented in random order. The hand is moved from side to side to show the alignment of the fingers. In these and all subsequent lessons, a pause follows presentation of each fingerspelled letter, word or sentence during which students viewing the films may write down or recite what was shown. A printed slide giving the meaning then appears.

The next 15 lessons provide practice in reading fingerspelled words and sentences at gradually increasing speeds. Several techniques were employed to give the student practice in adapting what he learns to real situations. The research staff who made the films used a variety of hands in them: students', deaf children's, staff members' hands with long fingers, short fingers, slender fingers, stubby fingers—and good fingerspellers as well as mediocre. Because, in actuality, one views a person from different positions, the staff filmed the lessons from several different angles.

*15. "Total Communication Series"—Southern Regional Media Center for the Deaf, 1814 Lake Avenue, Knoxville, Tennessee 37916.

This series of programs was developed for hearing parents who have children with hearing impairments. The presentation is simultaneous with speech, signs, fingerspelling, and various graphics included. Instruction in total communication, given for left and right-handed persons, includes many signs in wide use and local Eskimo signs. The series was produced in Alaska.

The series is composed of twenty-seven, twenty-minute programs (three per 1 hour of videotape). Keith Tolzin is the instructor and the program was produced by the Early Education Assistance Grant Program for Pre-school Hearing Impaired and funded by Media Services and Captioned Films, BEH/USOE.

The programs (9 hours long) are available from Southern Regional Media Center through a duplication program. Send to the Center enough blank videotape, plus return postage, for the program time. They will duplicate the programs requested and return the tapes. For more information contact the Southern Regional Media Center for the Deaf.

IMPORTANT NOTICE:

Information on availability and pricing of films was accurate at time of revision. However, some information may now be outdated. The Regional Media Centers are now, for example, no longer in existence. We suggest writing to the Specialized Office for Deaf and Hard of Hearing, University of Nebraska—Lincoln, Nebraska, Hall 175, Lincoln, Nebraska 68508.

INDEX

The illustrations are numbered consecutively, and each number below represents the corresponding number of the illustration in the text. No page numbers are given.

S

U

V

W

X

Y

Z